PRAISE FOR

GETTING THE JOB DONE

"These tips are the foundation of an effective methodology to simplify complex projects and drive measurable success."

—**Steve Garske PhD**, MSc, MBA, Chief Information Officer, Children's Hospital Los Angeles (CHLA)

"You owe it to yourself to read this book and draw from over 40 years of proven experience. Blending engaging stories with best practices, it's a guide you'll keep referencing throughout your project career."

—**Eric Brown**, VP of Membership, PMI LA Chapter

"This book is a thoughtful and practical framework for anyone interested in honing their skills in project management, whether you are seasoned professional or just starting out."

—**James P. Wellman**, CIO, Blanchard Valley Health System

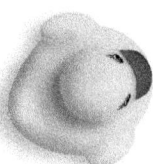

KEVIN TORF

PREPARED BY: T2 TECH GROUP

GETTING THE JOB DONE

PRACTICAL ADVICE AND REAL-WORLD ANECDOTES TO MANAGE SUCCESSFUL P.R.O.J.E.C.T.S.

AN INC.
ORIGINAL

An Inc. Original
New York, New York
www.anincoriginal.com

This work is being published under the An Inc. Original imprint by an exclusive arrangement with Inc. Magazine. Inc. Magazine and the Inc. logo are registered trademarks of Mansueto Ventures, LLC. The An Inc. Original logo is a wholly owned trademark of Mansueto Ventures, LLC.

Distributed by River Grove Books

Design and composition by Greenleaf Book Group and Brian Phillips
Cover design by Greenleaf Book Group and Brian Phillips
Cover image copyright Alex SG. Used under license from Shutterstock.com

Publisher's Cataloging-in-Publication data is available.

Print ISBN: 978-1-7360283-6-0

eBook ISBN: 978-1-7360283-7-7

First Edition

To Sue, Kyle, Gill, Jason, Caleigh,
and my extended T2 family

CONTENTS

Teamwork

Standards

PREFACE

The concept of this guide for entrepreneurs and project managers originated with Kevin Torf, managing partner at T2 Group in Los Angeles, California, whose forty-plus-year career in information technology design and management informed many of the project management tips it offers.

We present these tips via a brief, letter-by-letter framework—*P.R.O.J.E.C.T.S.* Each letter in this acronym represents one of the building blocks of project management: planning, reflection, organization, juggling, empowerment, communication, teamwork, and standards. Each of these blocks encompasses a critical area that every stakeholder, team leader, and team member confronts on a daily basis throughout their working life.

In the pages that follow, we break these blocks down one at a time. For each, we start by giving a quick preview of the block. We then turn to the tips—short, bite-sized pieces of advice that allow you and your team to make the most of each. Finally, we conclude each discussion with a case study from T2's client files. These studies show how we successfully leveraged a block during an actual project, leading to a cost-effective win for our client.

Here, a disclaimer and final acknowledgment is in order. These wins were the result of more than following a successful framework. Credit for them—and all that we do—ultimately belongs to T2's employees. Their passion cannot be put to paper, and there is no collection of tips, no matter how large, that can capture all the ways they have worked together to succeed. Nonetheless, we are confident that these tips have helped refine and support their work—and that teams who put them into practice will soon have new wins of their own.

ACKNOWLEDGMENTS

First, a special thanks to my wife, Sue. She has been with me from the beginning when I started my first company in 1980. Through the years she has helped me to express my thoughts and ideas and has always believed in me. I have evolved and learned so much through our relationship.

This book is dedicated to my partners, employees, and clients across all of T2's companies. Many of the tips in this book came about from working with my partners—Robert Konishi, Leigh Sleeman, and Kyle Torf—on different projects over the past decade. Each of them brought their own insights and perspectives to T2's various ventures, contributing something different that we have all learned from. Thanks is due to all the T2 project managers, engineers, subject-matter experts, and administrators who have contributed to the methodology the company practices today, and that is now articulated in this book. I would also like to thank the many people in T2 and the hired contractors, including Ian Bell, who have contributed writing support, corrected statements, helped articulate a point of view, and proofread this book.

Finally, I'd like to express my appreciation for all the clients across the nation that we've worked with and still serve. Your support built T2 from a team of two into the industry leader we are today. Your trust enabled us to find new approaches and your frank feedback guided the success of the P.R.O.J.E.C.T.S framework. This book is about sharing with others the lessons learned and the methodology that we created together. Thank you.

PLANNING

Every project begins with a blank slate: an empty space where the project's story must be written. What first fills that space is planning—a key driver in any project. Planning requires finding the correct balance between doing only the preparation you absolutely need to do versus thinking through every detail. Every situation calls for a different approach. However, when in doubt, get started and adjust. Create an idea and then allow it to evolve over time.

Marshaling a team to work on a project is an important part of the planning process. If you have the choice, select team members who can bring different, cross-functional skills and perspectives. This is not always possible, so you might need to adapt and distribute responsibilities based on other factors.

Once the team is selected, you and the other project managers—in conjunction with the stakeholder—must perform **triage** to determine which tasks will take priority during the project. Select a task for which you know the amount of effort required to complete it and establish it as a benchmark. Size up new tasks against the benchmark to gauge whether they will require more or less effort. Use this method to break down the project into a set of actionable items, determine defined milestones and estimates of hours required to achieve them, and calculate your progress. Define and build the **metrics** you will use to monitor the team's productivity.

A well-chosen team—one where responsibilities have been carefully distributed among all members—will be a key source of the information you need for planning. Solicit their input. Getting them to **weigh in** on how long they think tasks might take to accomplish has a host of advantages. For best results, be a leader, not a dictator. Don't tell your people **how to work**. As a project manager, your function is to communicate the objectives, as established by the stakeholder, that you expect your team to achieve.

While it has been opined that God is in the **details,** determining how much detail is required for a project is another key planning-phase consideration. Overcommitting to documentation that you cannot maintain or that does not provide any value can hurt productivity by siphoning time and resources away from the actual project. Such unnecessarily detailed work may be a manifestation of another pitfall to guard against when planning: the tendency to assign **busywork** to fill perceived downtime during a project. Instead, look to your team to maximize performance by establishing productive roles for everyone during every phase, thus giving the team a **purpose**.

Be flexible. If planning a particular phase of a project proves problematic, perhaps that phase is too big. Try breaking it down into **shorter iterations** or allow the team to focus on a smaller number of tasks that are more easily achieved. Lastly, sometimes things go awry and even the best laid plans fail, so it's smart to have a Plan B ready. Creating a backup plan, even if it is never used, also has far-reaching benefits (so long as your focus remains on the primary plan) because it helps your team become better prepared.

PROJECT TRIAGE

Developed in the eighteenth and nineteenth centuries during Napoleon's military campaigns, triage is the process of quickly determining the urgency of a soldier's treatment and subsequent emergency transport, based on the severity of their wounds.[1]

When planning a complex project, project managers must first perform triage by identifying its most critical elements, determining which elements will require the most time to accomplish, breaking them into smaller iterations, and identifying dependencies and critical needs so that they can be attacked first. When communicating with team members and stakeholders, provide real insight into what can be achieved within the scope, budget, and timeline. Don't tell stakeholders what you think they want to hear. Rather, tell them what they need to know.

What do you do when the project scope will not fit into the allocated budget and timeline?

Take a frank and realistic view of the tasks, with their associated time and costs, that the project scope requires. Then review with the stakeholders the recommended options that meet the project scope, timeline, and budget framework.

KEY TAKEAWAYS

✓ Assess what aspect of your project will take the most time.

✓ Decide what is most important to the success of your project.

✓ Communicate to your stakeholders what can be expected and completed in a given period of time.

✓ Prioritize tasks with dependencies that require lead time to coordinate.

KEEPING SCORE:
METRICS ARE VITAL TO PERFORMANCE

When the Ontario Soccer Association decided to stop keeping score for games with players twelve-and-under, public reaction was mixed. This decision wasn't based on some loud, overly competitive parents on the sidelines whose behavior was not in keeping with the spirit of the game. Leaders of the Association argued that the pressure to win games at the youngest ages was causing children to drop out of the sport, damaging skill development, and ultimately harming the health of Canada's national soccer program.[2]

Many people, like critics of the Association who charged that ending scoring would hurt competition, struggle with the idea of scoreless games. Isn't scoring necessary to measure achievement? For youth soccer, it may not be. But for project team members, scoring is essential: they need measurements to mark their progress. In fact, it's critical to break down a task or project into a set of actionable items that each person can correlate their work with, so they can understand what they finished and where they fell short, and more broadly, if they are achieving their goals.

Language is a critical part of establishing metrics. The more action items can be quantified with very specific language—or numbers, which are more exact than words—the easier it becomes to set and meet expectations with your team and with stakeholders.

Setting well-defined metrics is crucial for every team member's performance. Metrics and other benchmarks enable each member to identify their strengths and weaknesses. They learn what their work rate is, and you can better predict their productivity for future planning.

KEY TAKEAWAYS

✓ Break down every task or project into a series of measurable action items.

✓ Find a result or accomplishment that you can measure and validate that you have reached it.

✓ Use very specific language or numbers to make each action item quantifiable.

✓ Quantify with numbers when possible because words are often vague.

ASK YOUR TEAM TO WEIGH IN

The Pulitzer Prize–winning American playwright and caustic wit George S. Kaufman traveled to Hollywood in 1935 to write what would become one of the Marx Brothers' biggest hits, *A Night at the Opera*. When Kaufman arrived at MGM, studio head Irving Thalberg demanded to know when he could see an outline for the script.

"I don't know," replied Kaufman.

After Thalberg continued to badger Kaufman about when the script would be delivered, the playwright answered: "Mr. Thalberg, do you want it Wednesday or good?"[3]

When marshaling a team for work on a project, don't do what Thalberg did to Kaufman and badger them about when it will be done or how long it will take. Empower them; don't dictate terms. You can then discuss how you might change the scope of the work or the approach to fit your deadline and their capabilities. Forcing team members to adhere to timelines without their input is the start of a scenario ripe for failure. Even if you have a requirement that the project must be completed by a certain date, rather than begin the conversation with deliverables and timelines, ask your team members how long they think particular tasks might take to complete.

Respect and recognize that each person brings different attributes. Let each team member tell you what they are capable of doing and how long it will take. Some will work slower, some, faster. It's counterproductive to think that everybody should work the same way you do and at your pace.

KEY TAKEAWAYS

✓ Let team members commit to how long your project will take.

✓ Work with your team to learn how much they can get done in a given time period.

✓ Empower your team to decide how they will achieve their objectives.

✓ Leverage your team's expertise, and do not fool yourself into thinking that you know better than they do.

DON'T TELL YOUR PEOPLE HOW TO WORK

When he was chairman of Chrysler, Lee Iacocca summarized his approach to successful project management: "Right up front, tell people what you're trying to accomplish and what you're willing to sacrifice to accomplish it."[4]

But to follow Iacocca's example fully, keep in mind what else he had to say about his success: "I hire people brighter than me and then I get out of their way."[5] Yes, tell team members what the objective is and what you want the outcome to be. But it's just as important that you *not* plan the route they will take to get there. Get out of their way! Ideally, you want each team member to tell you how they're going to manage their own tasks.

There is a big difference between dictating and leading. As the project manager, your function is to communicate to your team the outcomes you expect based on the needs of your stakeholders. It is not your job to micromanage team members about how to do theirs.

Plan priorities—the desired outcomes—and then allow your team to engage. You will find that they are more fiercely committed because they are able to tell you how the goals and objectives you've targeted will be achieved. Gauge their achievements based on their results, rather than on their methods.

KEY TAKEAWAYS

- ✓ Allow your team to tell you how they will accomplish tasks and achieve objectives.
- ✓ Empower each team member to bring their expertise to the table and to use other team members' expertise to succeed.
- ✓ Evaluate your team by their accomplishments, not by the methodology they used to achieve them.

DETAILS CAN BE DEVILISH

James A. H. Murray, the first editor of one of the world's most comprehensive reference books, the *Oxford English Dictionary*, dealt with an unbelievable amount of documentation. To prepare the dictionary, volunteers from all over the world sent him quotations, each on its own separate slip of paper. In the end, Murray's scriptorium held five million slips.[6]

Unless you are creating a definitive dictionary, no project requires that level of documentation. Collecting too much information hurts productivity and draws time and energy away from the actual project. When it becomes obvious that such documentation is hard to maintain, it is usually abandoned. On the other hand, incomplete documentation is misleading and can paint an inaccurate picture of what happened.

Instead of being exhaustive, document only as necessary. Early in the planning process, identify what documentation can feasibly be maintained and include the updating of that documentation in the flow of the project plan. This ensures that at the end of the project, you will have an up-to-date, accurate account.

KEY TAKEAWAYS

✓ Identify the essential elements of what needs to be documented.

✓ Remember that overcommitting to documentation can be counterproductive.

✓ Only document to the extent you can maintain it.

✓ Build the updating of documents into the flow of the project plan.

INSTEAD OF BUSYWORK,
GIVE TEAM MEMBERS A PURPOSE

One of the greatest enemies of the U.S. military is boredom. When combat operations aren't going on, the armed forces employ busywork—forcing service members to attend pointless trainings, complete lackluster courses, and fill out unnecessary paperwork—to stop them from idling and becoming bored.[7]

It's a sensible strategy when you have masses of young, hormone-addled soldiers to keep out of trouble. But it's not how an organization that uses a team philosophy to get projects done should work. Some iterations may not require all of your team members, but this doesn't mean that they should be given busywork just to pass the time. Instead, have them focus on other tasks that have a purpose.

Which tasks? Answering that question is your team's job. As a group, they are responsible for ensuring each member has a purpose. Your team should keep in mind the range of options available for team members who have a lighter workload for a given phase. An otherwise idle team member might address a lingering action item, start laying the groundwork for the next iteration, or even temporarily go to another team that needs their skills. If your team collaborates closely and plans iterations together, each person will have a purpose.

The problem with many project teams' planning process is that they don't clearly think through each member's contribution. The result is often under-utilization and unnecessary busywork. Instead, when a team reviews goals and objectives together, solutions usually can be found that make the most of every person's time, even those who play a smaller part in the current iteration.

KEY TAKEAWAYS

✓ Plan the current iteration as a team, giving every member a purpose.

✓ Collaborate and align with one another on all the tasks that must be completed.

✓ Review the role of each member and find a job for them that will benefit your team.

✓ Be creative, and challenge team members to step outside their comfort zone if possible.

OVERWHELMED BY THE NEXT PHASE? TRY A SHORTER ONE

Ants are small in the animal kingdom, but they're also among its strongest members. A single ant can lift up to 5,000 times its own body weight, and an entire colony can move more than a ton of dirt as it builds its network of subterranean tunnels. Nothing, it seems, can stand in their way.

The reason ants can accomplish the seemingly impossible is because they work together as a team to move the dirt one grain at a time. It's an extraordinary example of teamwork and using an incremental approach to address big challenges—one that any team should bear in mind when they're struggling to plan an iteration of a project.

It's not unusual for teams to hit a wall and have trouble thinking through the tasks and roles that need to be assigned. One way to overcome that block is to have a smaller subgroup meet separately and brainstorm solutions, but that kind of splintering can be counterproductive to team cohesion. A better solution can be gleaned from the ants: help your team to understand what winning and success feel like by breaking projects into smaller, grain-sized parts and celebrating each small victory.

If your team is feeling overwhelmed by the next iteration of a project, that iteration might be too big. Discuss the challenges of the upcoming phase with them. Even if it's a two-week-long iteration, it may involve too many tasks and moving parts. Break it down and make it smaller. Consult the team, and if everyone is in agreement, try a one-week-long iteration instead to see if that works. Using smaller increments can help a team to get really focused on a set of achievable tasks.

KEY TAKEAWAYS

✓ If your team is struggling to plan, consider a shorter iteration. This forces the team to focus on a smaller number of tasks.

✓ Plan tasks that are reasonable and achievable within the iteration's timeframe.

✓ Give your team a boost along the way by setting small goals for them. Ensuring they do not overcommit during each iteration will increase engagement and improve morale.

PLAN FOR MURPHY'S LAW

One of the world's wisest sayings doesn't come from Socrates or the Buddha. The credit goes to Captain Edward A. Murphy Jr., an irritated Air Force engineer and the originator of Murphy's Law. In the late 1940s, Murphy was visiting a team testing the effects of large g-forces on the human body at Edwards Air Force Base. When the gauges Murphy provided were miswired by a technician and failed, the Captain angrily said, "If there's any way they can do it wrong, they will."[8]

What he said wasn't forgotten. It circulated around the base, becoming Murphy's Law as we know it today—"If anything can go wrong, it will." In later interviews, many on the base attributed their excellent safety record to heeding the law by preparing as much as possible for the potential problems every plan carries. Any team that puts complete faith in a single plan without making a backup defies Murphy's Law at its peril.

Even when a team has a solid strategy for tackling a project, it isn't a waste of time to consider what might go wrong. Statistically, the odds are against an outcome that's error-free. When teams decline to consider a Plan B, and even, possibly, a Plan C, they put themselves in a very poor position with their sponsors or other stakeholders. When an accident happens—and one will—they will look careless and irresponsible.

There's no need to obsess about negative consequences, but there are good reasons for teams to consider backup plans. It forces them to view a project in terms of risk. Even if nothing else comes of it, having a discussion about potential risks helps teams have a more complete understanding of the project. Encourage open communication and exploration of all the options.

KEY TAKEAWAYS

✓ Consider and plan for potential problems—odds are that there will be one.

✓ Create a Plan B to help your team be better prepared overall. Developing a Plan B allows the team to consider all of the risks that might affect a project.

✓ Create an environment where all options can be considered by your team.

JUST START SOMETHING ALREADY!

President and Commander of the Allied Forces in Europe during World War II Dwight D. Eisenhower once said: "In preparing for battle, I have always found that plans are useless, but planning is indispensable."[9] As a project manager, starting without any planning is risky, but planning every detail may be wasteful. The key is to begin with the right balance. Prioritize goals and tasks, and plan enough to account for budget, schedule, risks, and dependencies. Start, then learn and adapt. If you focus on lessons learned and make process improvements as you go forward, a balance between planning and action will be achieved.

Establish a balance between intensive preplanning and the actual commencement of a project. Account for risks and dependencies, get started, and then incorporate lessons learned as the project progresses.

KEY TAKEAWAYS

✓ Do enough planning to understand your goals, objectives, risks, and dependencies so you can get started.

✓ Consider costs and schedule in your initial plan.

✓ Plan what is critical, prioritizing goals and tasks.

✓ Once the scope is understood, launch the project and adapt as you go.

CASE STUDY

SUMMARY

To find the right balance between doing too much planning or too little, you must first understand the business you are involved in. Know the overall scope, budget, timeline, objectives, and risks of each project, and be cognizant of how quickly things could change during the course of a project due to unforeseeable events. If you overplan, when the time comes to execute those plans, they may be obsolete and hours of effort will have been wasted. There is no value in planning long term for something that will change in the short term. But too little planning can lead to not anticipating avoidable problems. Good planning comes down to determining the level of detail needed for the plan to succeed while still keeping the project moving forward.

PROBLEM

A client had outsourced the hosting of their electronic health record software to a third party. After outsourcing, the client encountered problems—including project delays, data loss, and system outages—that resulted in a loss of confidence from the physicians, nurses, and executive leadership. After deciding to bring their electronic health record software in-house, the client chose to work with T2 to manage the migration. Ensuring that third-party hosting issues did not follow the application in-house could only be achieved with careful planning at every level.

SOLUTION

A coordinated plan with clearly defined milestones was key to meeting the project's deadline. T2 broke up the project into multiple deliverables under different teams, infrastructure, application, historical data, and other disciplines. This approach provided the necessary level of detail and oversight so that each team could focus on its own responsibilities. The final operational transition was planned down to the minute, and this resulted in only a brief planned downtime followed by full system availability. This enabled the IT organization to regain the confidence and support of the executive leadership and minimized the effect of the transition on clinical staff, allowing them to stay focused on providing excellent patient care.

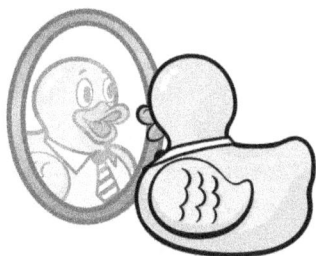

REFLECTION

When the pace and requirements of your project are extreme, it may feel counterintuitive to stop and reflect on how far you've come and where you are in terms of the **original scope** and **ultimate goals**. But it is under these conditions that some of your greatest insights can occur.

Indeed, the value of reflection can hardly be overstated. Reflection is crucial for effective project management and is a vital part of the Agile philosophy. First articulated in 2001 in "The Agile Manifesto," it calls for the development of systems in short, frequent phases with constant evaluation and improvements to promote customer satisfaction. Reflection reveals which **patterns** have proven successful during the course of a project, and which have not. It allows for the flexibility to make improvements to subsequent phases and adjustments to accommodate an **ever-changing business landscape**.

Regular reassessments by your team can, rather than slowing a project down, actually enable **more frequent cycles** that will help them align more closely with a business situation in flux. Such cycles also foster more communication between the team and its sponsor. While a **delay** can put your team in a difficult position with stakeholders, reflection, in its various forms, will allow you and your team to better understand what stakeholders are looking for and to develop better ways of achieving these objectives. Reflective assessments provide insights and information that a project manager can use to optimize a team's performance and reevaluate expectations. It's also important to reflect on how you develop the narratives that you use to communicate the project's progress. Taking time to choose the right words helps ensure that you **frame** your message appropriately.

A form of reflection by and for the team, **retrospective meetings** are opportunities for **growth** and **improvement**. Regardless of the outcome, every project needs retrospective checkpoints where all discussion remains **privileged information** shared only between team members. The team and the project stand to benefit from discussing both failures and triumphs.

Like a project, a business can reap the rewards of reflection as well. Frequent reflection sparks innovation, reveals errors quickly, and allows for a business to respond, recover, and **shift direction**. Industry changes require adaptation, so to keep thriving, businesses must **continually learn** and thrive.

E.T. PHONE HOME

Movie lovers remember the lovable E.T. character who had an unplanned adventure on Earth. Regardless of his exciting experiences and new friendships, he remained focused on his mission: to "phone home" and, ultimately, return to his planet.

As a project manager, it's critical you maintain E.T.-like focus on the original scope of your project and regularly reflect on it. Employ a cadence that allows you and your team to reflect, improve, and optimize your project's scope as needed. This review strengthens your team's performance by validating how effectively they're moving toward the original objective. It allows the team to assess operations, tactics, strategies, and more to determine if new developments present a need to adjust the original objective.

Utilizing the power of project iterations can make productivity soar, yet it can also take you in unanticipated directions. How do you ensure your course stays aligned with the project's original objectives and stakeholder needs?

Step back for reflection and reassessment. These powerful tools sustain progress and keep a project moving in the right direction, allowing you to reevaluate your objectives.

KEY TAKEAWAYS

✓ Engage your team and stakeholders in the reflection and assessment process.

✓ While reflecting, revisit the original scope of the project and identify any necessary changes to it.

✓ Manage change versus fighting it as you refine your goals and objectives.

REVISIT ORIGINAL GOALS OFTEN

Long before the creation of electronic navigation systems, sailors used manual dead reckoning to guide their ships. The navigator would measure the distance and map out a course to a destination from his home port. Each day's progress was marked on a chart to help him understand the ship's movement in relation to home and how much the ship may have drifted from its original course.

Today, with GPS, it's much harder for a ship to go off course or become lost at sea than in the past. But even though manual dead reckoning is no more, sailors haven't changed in one respect: they still keep a constant eye on the home port as they move farther ahead on their journey. It's the same in any project. A project's original goals are your team's home port, and it's vital to look back on them regularly to make sure they are still on course.

It isn't unusual to deviate from project goals and need a course correction: change is a common part of any project. What is problematic, though, is when a team decides to reinterpret the original goals to justify what they're doing or where they are currently. That practice undermines the team's credibility and makes it appear as if they are trying to avoid taking responsibility for problems that may have occurred.

Keep your team focused on the current definition of the goals you have been asked to achieve. If the goal has been changed or adjusted by the stakeholder, that's a different story. Stakeholder changes must be followed—but be sure to record and document when a change in goals has been requested by the stakeholder so that everyone is clear about it and there is no mystery later as to what happened.

KEY TAKEAWAYS

- ✓ Remind yourself of, and reinforce, project objectives often.
- ✓ Check that your team is meeting the project's goals and objectives.
- ✓ Keep your entire team focused on what is necessary to achieve the goals and any changes a stakeholder makes to them along the way.

NARCISSUS GOT A BAD RAP

Greek mythology chronicles the demise of the demigod Narcissus, who obsessed over his own reflection in a pool of water with tragic results. Many ancient superstitions from around the world purport that it is risky, unlucky, or even fatal to gaze at one's own reflection.

In project management, reflection offers great and beneficial power. When team members reflect together, it provides a robust tool to encourage progress through structured change. The team assesses their approach and learns how to improve their effectiveness. It is in reflection that some of a team's greatest actionable insights can be found.

Regular sessions to review the project's work status may be seen by some team members as a waste of time. Why should they be held when moving forward with the greatest speed possible is a top priority?

Reflection enables a team to evaluate what's working and what's not, and to apply lessons learned through iterative change.

KEY TAKEAWAYS

✓ Encourage your team to understand the value of reflection.

✓ Schedule team sessions dedicated to reflection.

✓ Look for patterns that have proven to be successful.

✓ Eliminate, adapt, or change unsuccessful patterns as appropriate.

A FRAME MAKES A BIG DIFFERENCE

Back in 2007, the art world buzzed with the news that a portrait of Lorenzo de' Medici by Raphael was going up for auction. Raphael's work is in and of itself spectacular. But the splendid gold frame around it makes Lorenzo's figure glow with even more warmth and richness.

Picture frames affect how people view a painting. Whether simple or ornate, a frame can change our entire perspective. The same can be said about how you frame your team meetings. For example, how do you refer to checkpoint meetings? Do you describe them as "postmortem" or "retrospective"? The words you choose affect your team's perceptions. What you decide to call a meeting sends a signal about whether it will be a fault-finding session or a productive conversation about what worked and what didn't.

Take great care when communicating with team members and stakeholders alike. Always be mindful of how you couch your messages—because what you want to say could easily get lost if you don't frame it appropriately.

KEY TAKEAWAYS

✓ Thoughtfully prepare your presentations.

✓ Clearly communicate the purpose of your meetings.

✓ Verify the content and quality of what you are going to say before you say it.

✓ Make sure that what you say is understandable to everyone.

WAITING ISN'T ALWAYS A VIRTUE

In 2005, Amazon Prime was born. Originally, the subscription program enabled consumers in the US to receive free two-day shipping on eligible items in exchange for payment of an annual fee. Dozens of factors have influenced the success of Amazon, including a knowledge of consumer behavioral psychology, which has helped the company become a leading innovator, deliver great results, and provide superior customer service.

Amazon understands that waiting affects consumers and their purchasing habits. Waiting is also a challenge for any team project, especially when delays arise that are outside of the team's control. When a delay happens, it's natural to want to hit the pause button until more information is available: no one wants to risk making important decisions without all the facts. And yet your team's work need not grind to a halt. Resist the temptation to put off scheduled meetings until all task results are available. As logical as it may seem, waiting for complete results is not always the most productive course. Timelines are affected, tasks go unfinished, and the team might run out of time if any last-minute fixes are needed.

If you're faced with a lengthy pause during an iteration, don't fill in the time with busywork. Instead, take the opportunity to schedule a team reflection session and draw from your backlog, which enumerates all the tasks that need to be done to complete the project. Don't forget to keep lines of communication open with everyone. During delays, it is critically important that you are open and transparent with all parties about the situation.

KEY TAKEAWAYS

✓ Communicate how delays will affect the project.

✓ Only cancel meetings if absolutely necessary. Even if a task is delayed, your team needs to stay informed.

✓ Use delays as a learning opportunity for your team and have a retrospective meeting.

✓ If delays occur, use this time by drawing tasks from your backlog.

SHARPENING THE SAW

A woodcutter, the story goes, was having trouble felling a tree. A young man walking by stopped to ask him what he was doing. The woodcutter replied that he was cutting down the tree. The young man told the woodcutter—who looked exhausted—to take a break and sharpen his saw. The woodcutter shot back, exasperated, "I don't have time! Can't you see I'm busy?"

A woodcutter needs to stop every now and again to sharpen his saw—otherwise, he will not be effective. It's no different for a team. Reflection is a vital part of the Agile philosophy, but it is often overlooked by teams. The oversight is understandable. It's natural, especially when a team is finishing a highly successful iteration, to want to keep the momentum going and flow right into the next one, not slam on the brakes.

Taking time for reflection about a just-completed iteration, however, can actually lead to even better results in the next. Stopping briefly—to reinforce the methods that worked well, and discuss what could have been done differently or better—has been shown to actually boost a team's cohesiveness and future capabilities.

Agile principles call for short iterations to enable teams to spend time reflecting on member dynamics and performance without introducing lengthy delays into the project process. The most effective teams include time for feedback in their planning for the next iteration.

KEY TAKEAWAYS

✓ Consider different approaches to achieving the same task.

✓ Evaluate every iteration to identify what was successful and what could have been better.

✓ Use reflection to determine how to improve team performance during your next iteration.

REFLECT ON YOUR BUSINESS DIRECTION

YouTube, the largest video-sharing site in the world, did not start that way. In 2005, YouTube was launched as a dating website. It offered users twenty dollars to post videos of themselves. That approach failed, and users began to post whatever videos they felt like posting. The founders pivoted, embraced the idea, and revamped the website and the company. Today, YouTube has over two billion users.

YouTube's decision to change its business model underscores the importance of periodically reevaluating your business and deciding if it still meets your goals. If it doesn't, then it's time to replace it with something that will. Good project management not only encourages such reflection at the project and team levels, but also considers it a must for every business.

Is our model still the right one? Is this still what the business landscape wants? Market demands change quickly, and it's critical to reflect often about what you're doing and why you're doing it. Reflecting on a company's goals improves both its productivity and its long-term direction.

A business model and sense of mission that are too rigid can be dangerous and lead to a dead end. No one can know the future, but reflection leaves room for the kinds of flexibility and adaptation necessary in a business landscape prone to disruptions, especially those caused by new technologies.

KEY TAKEAWAYS

- ✓ Recognize that regularly reflecting on your business goals is a necessity.
- ✓ Accept that business goals aren't permanent, but that they need to keep up with a changing market.
- ✓ Use frequent reflection to ensure that project results are in sync with the needs of your industry.

STAY ON COURSE WITH
MORE FREQUENT REVIEW CYCLES

Back in 1929, famed flying ace Jimmy Doolittle was the first person to fly blind. Using radio navigation, an altimeter, an artificial horizon display, and several other instruments, he was able to fly, take off, and land without ever looking out from under a fabric cockpit hood.[10] Pilots today rely on such instruments because the skies are constantly changing, and these instruments supply crucial data right when it's needed most.

When you're working in a fast-changing industry—software development or healthcare, for instance—market conditions can change just as quickly as the skies. What worked yesterday may not serve your business model right now. While a pilot has flight instruments to help him adjust, your team has something just as reliable: more frequent review cycles.

More review cycles enable a team to stay closely aligned with a changing business situation. Not all businesses change quickly and need short iterations and rapid reviews. But for many, having a two-week-long iteration strikes a good balance between the extremes of week-long and month-long iterations. While week-long iterations may move too fast for some, iterations of a month or longer run the risk of proceeding too far without the ability to check the gauges and course correct early enough to avoid wasted effort.

Short iterations and fast review cycles mean that a finished project will more accurately reflect the current business, not what it looked like when the project started. Fast review cycles also are helpful to the team because they provide prompt feedback that fits the current situation. More frequent reviews also enable the team to communicate more often with sponsors, which can be invaluable, especially if there are problems that need to be corrected.

KEY TAKEAWAYS

✓ Keep review cycles short—this will help you keep better track of changing business needs.

✓ The longer you wait for review cycles, the more that can (and will) go wrong.

✓ Keep your team on track and aligned with prompt feedback to ensure success.

KEEP RETROSPECTIVE MEETINGS TO YOURSELVES

One of the greatest marketing campaigns in the history of tourism used the famous tagline "What Happens in Vegas Stays in Vegas." To boost its sagging tourism numbers, the city hired a marketing team in 2003 to rebrand itself from Sin City, world capital of gambling and corruption, to a place where people—families, too—go to have fun, enjoy some freedom, and leave their troubles behind.

The campaign was wildly successful. Since then, the famous phrase has been applied to any situation where a little secrecy is required, be it a bachelorette party, a night out with friends—or a team meeting.

Why is discretion required for successful meetings? Because team members need to feel that they're not being judged or watched by management during these events. Once assured of this, they're more likely to participate, share, and fully engage, whether they are in a retrospective meeting, or planning for the next iteration.

Meetings can be invaluable bonding and learning opportunities for teams—if team members feel comfortable. They need reassurance that they can freely interact at these meetings without consequences. They need to know that everyone will be treated as equals and that remarks won't be shared with management. In other words, what happens in the meeting stays in the meeting.

KEY TAKEAWAYS

✓ Encourage and support team bonding.

✓ Protect retrospective meetings and other team meetings as times for sharing free from the eyes and judgment of management and stakeholders.

✓ Information discussed in a meeting is for the team's benefit only as they work through an issue or problem.

EVOLVE AND THRIVE

An anonymous poem, often ascribed to the great Lebanese-American poet Kahlil Gibran, speaks of a river trembling in fear before entering the sea. After coursing through mountains and villages over many miles, the river is afraid of disappearing forever into the vastness of the sea. But then the river realizes that by entering the sea, it won't cease to be—it will become the sea.

Evolution occurs through innovation, and that often means taking chances, something most people are reluctant to do. But without risk there is minimal reward—and absolutely no evolution in managing projects or situations dynamically. Making mistakes is part of the evolutionary process, but if they are caught early, damage can be minimized and learning can be enhanced.

As you innovate and evolve, conduct regular retrospective meetings—even when things seem to be going right. It's not about finding fault, but rather about learning and thriving, applying insights learned to better the current project and those that come after it. At the same time, reevaluate to make sure you are still on course to achieve the desired objectives.

Evolution doesn't happen by repeating the same tasks or processes over and over. Improvement, driven by knowledge and experience, occurs when you consistently look for different ways to accomplish the tasks at hand.

KEY TAKEAWAYS

- ✓ Always look for opportunities to improve existing methods.
- ✓ Don't be afraid to take risks in order to learn. It's OK to be wrong if you catch the mistake quickly through regular retrospective meetings.
- ✓ Hold retrospective meetings to understand how to improve and reevaluate your objectives and make sure that you are meeting them.

CASE STUDY

SUMMARY

Reflecting on what you've done well and what you could have done better allows you to put that knowledge into practice. It's *not* about finding fault. Reflection is especially valuable when a project requires repetitive tasks. Bear in mind, however, that the process should not just be project-specific. It should also include the behavior of you and your team, the content you are charged with delivering to the client, and even your work environment. Reflection, to be truly successful, must be a consistent, oft-repeated ritual.

PROBLEM

A client needed to transition all clinical staff from standard PCs with generic logins to a brand-new virtual desktop infrastructure while minimizing disruption to hospital staff and patient care.

SOLUTION

T2 created a multiphase rollout plan that transitioned one department at a time using a repeatable process and template. At the end of each deployment, T2 consultants interviewed department leadership on what could be done to improve the transition, and then held a retrospective meeting with the project team to assess this input. This allowed the team to improve on all aspects of the rollouts, including coordination, scheduling, training, device replacement, go-live activities, system issues, and support. After using this approach with several departments, T2 was able to limit the impact of subsequent deployments on the staff of other departments and enhance the user experience by improving every aspect of the process.

REFLECTION

ORGANIZATION

Regardless of how much or how little you plan, do not mistake planning for being organized. Organization creates discipline and governance. An organized team will repeat its successes and deliver predictably excellent results time and again. Being organized can significantly increase productivity and provides a path to quicker results.

Organization is pivotal for any successful project. Without it, imbalance and chaos ensue at every level. When organizing a project, the first step is to quantify and accept the **three key constraints** involved in every project: time, scope, and budget. Remaining aware of the delicate relationship between these constraints ensures that your team works within them.

Ultimately, all organizational imperatives exist to satisfy the **stakeholder**, so the second step is to anticipate your customer's needs and build your plan around making sure they are satisfied. After that, break down the project into **short steps** that, by their very nature, provide a trusty roadmap for the work ahead and **determine who on your team will do what**.

Once the project commences, **check-in meetings** with your team will help you spot potential problems that might undermine organizational imperatives. For these meetings—as well as all business meetings and presentations—remember that effective, organized communication calls for preparation, an **audience-focused approach**, and safeguards against **wasting time**. The best presentations connect with listeners and give them clear, meaningful takeaways.

Organizational tools can be invaluable for ushering a project to completion. However, make sure the tools you use do not end up using you. Tools are meant to be helpful, not make a situation worse.

Finally, be certain to define **finished** clearly in your planning. Completing a project in short iterations minimizes having to revisit a lot of work you've already done.

ACCEPT CONSTRAINTS

Chuck Yeager, an American test pilot and US Air Force officer, was the first man to break the sound barrier. For Yeager and other legendary test pilots, success required paying scrupulous attention to many factors affecting their flights at high altitudes. Ignore these factors, and a pilot would suddenly find the basic laws of aerodynamics allied against him, sending his plane out of control and "tumbling . . . end over end like a brick."[11] At that moment, failure was guaranteed, and with it, death.

Your team's performance may not be a matter of life or death, but their success or failure does hinge on paying attention to important factors. While Yeager and his fellow pilots battled g-forces and thin air, your team struggles with three important constraints in every project: time, scope, and budget.

Each team must face the fact that it's difficult to optimize all three factors at the same time. If you try to save time and money, for example, you'll probably sacrifice the project's scope. If you decide to expand the project's scope, the required time and money will change too. Rather than fight against the triple constraint, understand its implications.

It's the team's responsibility to set expectations up front with stakeholders about the effect of project changes. Be mindful that changing any constraint affects the other two. Therefore, a delicate balance must always be maintained between a project's timeframe, scope, and budget. And don't forget to incorporate a method of evaluation to ensure the team is staying within these constraints.

KEY TAKEAWAYS

✓ Set clear objectives with stakeholders regarding what decisions are most important.

✓ Minimize time, money, and scope risks through frequent communication among stakeholders.

✓ Don't conflate scope with quality. Sacrificing quality should always be the last resort, with the consequences fully understood.

✓ Work with stakeholders at the outset to determine their flexibility regarding time, scope, and budget.

GO THE DISTANCE ONE STEP AT A TIME

According to exercise scientist Greg McMillan, there are three types of runners: endurance monsters, combo runners, and speedsters.[12] Which are you? In the world of distance running, marathoners fall squarely into the first category: "the more miles we log on a weekly basis, the better" is their mantra. As a general rule, most runners are able to adjust between long and short distances, making them combo runners. Speedsters, though, are a rare breed. They're the true champions of the short game. With quick bursts of speed, they easily leave everyone in the dust in races of five kilometers or less.

It's tempting for teams to go after the big end result in a project like a marathoner, but a better strategy is inspired by the speedsters. Forget the overall goal and focus instead on shorter bursts, or iterations. If you do, you'll get the best feedback and the information you need to complete the project successfully.

This approach can help a team that is feeling intimidated by a project's overall goals. Breaking up the project into shorter tasks will give the team more confidence for the work ahead and curtail needless worrying about how they will get there.

It's often difficult for the team—and especially for those who are stakeholders but non-performers—to see how they're going to get from start to finish on a project. The shorter the task, the more accurate the estimates of the effort required to accomplish it are likely to be and the more achievable the expected result is. Shorter sprints also bring other advantages: a lower cost of failure, more immediate data, and useful feedback.

KEY TAKEAWAYS

✓ Break up projects into shorter iterations.

✓ Focus on the current iteration only: progress is built one task at a time.

✓ Use regular communication to keep your team focused on immediate tasks.

✓ Involve hands-on stakeholders in the testing, feedback, and planning needed to build the roadmap for the next iteration.

THE STRENGTH OF EACH TEAM MEMBER IS THE TEAM

Just one cyclist mounts the podium to accept the Tour de France trophy, but it takes a whole team to get him there. One member of the team who epitomizes this is the domestique—a cyclist who functions as an all-purpose helper. The domestique's responsibilities include everything from bringing supplies of water or food from the team car to riding in front of the team leader to buffer him from the wind and other riders. As a CNN headline once put it, "'Domestiques' prove there is no I in team."

Just like in the Tour de France, every team is made up of individuals—indispensable cogs in an overall machine—who work toward achieving goals. It's important to remember, however, that those shared goals ultimately must be accomplished together.

Achieving team unity comes down to having an overarching strategy for the project that details what each team member needs to do to make it successful—just as the domestiques in the Tour de France know their role is to help their leader get across the finish line first.

Although the strengths of individual team members are crucial to project success, remember that everyone on the team should be working in tandem to achieve all the goals targeted in the strategic plan.

KEY TAKEAWAYS

✓ Select the role that each team member will perform in the context of the overall strategy.

✓ Realize that, ultimately, the project and process is about the team working toward one unified and primary goal.

✓ Encourage the team to work together on a strategy that they all can agree on.

ORGANIZATION

BE WARY OF WASTING TIME

"Remember that time is money." Benjamin Franklin didn't invent this message, but he turned it into a saying that the average Joe can understand and appreciate. Ever since its appearance in his 1748 essay "Advice to a Young Tradesman," that time-conscious sentiment has been engrained in the American psyche.

Franklin's practical attitude has found a home in today's Agile philosophy, especially in the practice of breaking down big projects into smaller iterations and carefully budgeting time. Franklin was known to rigorously schedule his days to avoid any waste. If he were alive today and observing a typical team meeting, he might be a little disappointed: too often meetings drift because of poorly defined objectives, wasting precious time.

The key to a successful meeting is asking and fixating on specific questions. Is there a problem with the timeline? Do we need to revise it? Are there unexpected costs in the current iteration? And so on. Meetings shouldn't be drawn-out affairs, especially when a few specific issues need addressing. Avoid vague meeting agendas to spare your team unnecessary waste and to move them forward in a positive, productive way.

Free-flowing brainstorming sessions can be valuable in the planning process, and they're good for team interaction. But not every meeting works this way. Scheduling meetings without a defined agenda and clear action items wastes time and squanders team productivity.

KEY TAKEAWAYS

✓ Create very clear action items for team meetings.

✓ Start on time, even if all team members aren't there.

✓ Find an optimal time for meetings when members are most likely to be energized and motivated.

✓ To incentivize team members to stay focused, promise to end early if all action items are addressed.

CHECK IN WITH YOUR TEAM DAILY

At the dawn of the twenty-first century, a driver heading to an unfamiliar location was likely armed with just two things: a copy of the *Thomas Guide* map book and the latest traffic reports on the radio. However, there was still a good chance that she'd face unexpected congestion or make a wrong turn and end up at a dead end.

Today, thanks to Google Maps, Waze, and other driving apps, drivers not only have a clear route to their destination. They also get real-time reports on actual hazards and alternate routes to avoid traffic and save time. This technology enables drivers to dynamically predict the journey ahead and change the route if necessary. For a project manager, that function is performed by a crucial tool in any project process: the daily morning meeting.

Substitute your team for the car, the day's task for the destination, and the meeting itself for the driving app, and you get the idea. Daily short meetings are essential to spotting problems that might come up in real time with that day's tasks. These quick meetings aren't meant to be comprehensive: they aren't forums for making big decisions or having lengthy conversations. Their purpose is simply to identify daily goals and any potential roadblocks to achieving them.

Even when a particular day's challenges may not involve everyone, the whole team should still join the quick meeting. It's important that everyone understands the situation, even if their specific duties aren't affected.

KEY TAKEAWAYS

- ✓ Meet every morning to identify daily tasks to achieve that day's goals.
- ✓ Daily meetings can also enable the team to pick the best route by identifying roadblocks.
- ✓ Keep these meetings short and focused.

WHEN SPEAKING, FOCUS ON YOUR AUDIENCE

When a speaker is invited to give a TED Talk, they receive a list of the TED Commandments. Most people who give these talks—which have become the gold standard for what a great public speech should be—aren't born storytellers or professional speakers. For TED Talk organizers, though, anyone can be coached to act like one.

Behind the humor of the commandments—the first one is "Thou Shalt Not Simply Trot Out Thy Usual Shtick"—is a practical lesson for any situation, whether it's a quick daily check-in or a presentation to a stakeholder. Make sure, TED Talk organizers say, that your remarks are audience-focused. The best presentations connect with listeners and communicate something meaningful.

The next time you're tapped to address an audience, remember that you're there to relay information on behalf of your team. Study reports and other related material in advance. Get to the point, and don't waste time. Too often speakers digress or offer explanations no one asked for. Nothing exudes more confidence than a focused, direct speaker. And the secret to such success boils down to one simple word: preparation.

The more you can train your mind to understand that you are presenting for your team, the more you will take the focus—and pressure—off yourself. Chances are, it will help you feel more comfortable and deliver a better presentation.

KEY TAKEAWAYS

✓ Prepare as much as is practical for meetings and all business presentations.

✓ Present information relevant to your audience.

✓ Be direct and clear with the information presented—this builds trust in your audience.

✓ Avoid unnecessary explanations—don't offer one unless asked.

DON'T LET TOOLS USE YOU

During the Siege of Syracuse in 213 BCE, the great mathematician Archimedes devised a series of defensive tools to keep the city from falling into Roman hands, including a huge crane to overturn ships and a battery of catapults that could inflict heavy losses at any range.[13] Despite the effectiveness of his innovations, the city eventually fell to the Romans, and Archimedes was killed. Syracuse's defenses might have been virtually impregnable, but no defense could stop the Syracusans' worst enemy: themselves. In the end, a pro-Roman faction gave up the city voluntarily.

Never let tools govern you by allowing them to drive your methodology or your productivity. Since time is one of the key constraints on every project, it's important to make sure the tools you use help you make the most of your time.

Sometimes workers fixate on things that don't necessarily contribute to the desired results. By focusing on extraneous issues, such as learning how to use a new tool, they may lose sight of the fact that the goal is not being accomplished. If a task will take an hour to complete, don't spend a day or a week learning how to use a new tool that may eventually help you accomplish it. Remember not to neglect other disciplines in favor of new tools. In some cases, even writing a note longhand is the most efficient option if learning a new digital tool would take an excessive amount of time.

If you have information that is subpar and you stray from solid disciplines, tools can actually make a situation worse. In addition, the extra time and resources needed to implement a tool may result in overlooking a task critical to the project's success.

KEY TAKEAWAYS

✓ Don't let tools govern your methodology.

✓ Include the time and effort it will take to learn how to use any new tools in your effort estimates.

✓ Simpler tools such as handwritten notes may be the most efficient method.

PUT YOURSELF IN YOUR CUSTOMER'S SHOES

One of the most enlightening proverbs in the American lexicon warns: "Don't judge a man until you have walked a mile in his shoes." Or, less metaphorically: you never really know someone until you understand things from their point of view.

When fixated on the details of a project and getting it done on time and on budget, a project manager can lose sight of the end user they are doing it for. In the rush to get the job done efficiently, the human element—the customer—is sometimes lost. Therefore, it's important to predicate all your actions on the value your finished product will bring its end user.

The best way to determine if you are meeting your customer's needs is to assemble a focus group of three to four people who can generate a consensus about what will be required to satisfy the customer's needs. Together, they can explore different options that will bring that about and settle on the best one.

The best way to satisfy customers is to anticipate what they need and expect from your efforts on their behalf. To accomplish that, adopt their mindset. Don't just listen and react: understand their perspective and where they are coming from.

KEY TAKEAWAYS

✓ Put yourself into the mind of your customer to determine what they need.

✓ Base all your actions on how they will affect the customer.

✓ Explore a variety of options for how you will solve your customer's problems.

✓ Build a focus group to reach a consensus on what will be required for customer satisfaction.

FINISH AND BE DONE

In his landmark Broadway musical *Sunday in the Park with George*, composer-cum-lyricist Stephen Sondheim devotes a song called "Finishing the Hat" to the protagonist, French Pointillist painter Georges Seurat. It's about the artist's single-minded dedication to completing the hat in his painting before moving on to other parts of the canvas or, for that matter, anything else in his life. The lyrics of the song emphasize the importance of finishing what you start.

Finishing segments of a project needs to be a definitive process. It means not having to revisit the work you've already done. It is important to understand the concept of *done*—much like Sondheim's Seurat knew when he was finished with the hat. Partitioning a project into smaller segments that are completed one at a time makes it easier to document, test, and validate those segments before moving to the next project phase. Then, as you near completion, the various building blocks have already had their quality assured.

People often don't know when they're done because they haven't defined what the term really means. The meaning of done needs to be articulated before tasks are even begun. Bringing each segment or phase of a project to completion eliminates the need for reworking unfinished components later on and, in the process, saves valuable time.

KEY TAKEAWAYS

- ✓ Define what you are going to do before you start so you will understand when you are done.
- ✓ Commit and focus on each task until you are done.
- ✓ Make each task a finished product so you never have to revisit that task.

CASE STUDY

SUMMARY

A well-organized workplace has structure. It has firm disciplines in place that delineate the role and area of responsibility of each team member as well as the role of the stakeholder. Organization provides a foundation that team members can lean on, and it sets a framework to streamline communication and decision making.

PROBLEM

T2 was retained by a client to collaborate on and implement a new approach for managing the client's projects. Working with the client's teams, we identified the absence of a standardized process for the intake and management of scope-change requests. This led to an inability to categorize and respond to these requests properly due to missing information and a lack of central coordination and prioritization.

SOLUTION

T2 introduced a hybrid methodology based on Agile principles, implementing a new organizational structure that effectively managed workflows and the decision-making process. All scope-change requests were funneled through this new process, streamlining how requests came in and providing a single source for identifying the key stakeholder for each request. Additionally it made clear which team was to fulfill the requests. Once that organizational structure was in place, T2 was able to build the Agile structures requested and helped the client complete multiple initiatives much faster than they had thought possible.

JUGGLING

The more balls in the air, the more fun it is to watch—that is, if you're a juggler. But when a team is working on a project, juggling can quickly devolve into disaster if you're not careful. To maximize progress on any project, it's important to orchestrate your team's workflow based on an **honest, carefully considered assessment** of what they can reasonably achieve. Prioritize the tasks and oversee the flow to avoid having too many balls in the air at one time. This will help you avoid **multitasking**: the worst kind of juggling, as it reduces productivity and leads to mistakes and underperformance.

To earn their trust, demonstrate to stakeholders that focusing on **one "ball" at a time** leads to success—the more focused your team is on one task, the more quickly all tasks will be completed. Make sure your team targets **current stakeholder objectives**. Keep in mind that the deeper you go into the **details of a task**, the more accurate your predictions will be about how long it will take to accomplish the work ahead.

One of the best ways for a project manager to minimize the number of balls in the air is to **prepare for the unexpected.** Bringing the team together with key stakeholders to brainstorm potential risks and changes that may lie ahead will help you anticipate them. When faced with change, **coach team members** through it, keep iterations short, and emphasize completing one task before moving on to the next.

Time management goes hand in hand with successfully juggling aspects of a project, and **even small losses add up**. A simple tool, the meeting agenda, can make the most of the time available and help keep everyone on course. A prerequisite for every meeting, agendas set boundaries, keep team members on topic, and maintain focus for the group. Such singular focus throughout the life of a project will not only ensure productive meetings—it will also prevent you from dropping the ball on key deliverables.

HONESTY IS ALWAYS THE BEST POLICY

The "Big Dig," officially known as the Central Artery/Tunnel Project, in Boston, Massachusetts, went over budget by more than ten billion dollars and was delayed by eight years.[14, 15] Problems leading to these overruns included design flaws, the use of incorrect materials, environmental issues, weak soil, poor planning, and underestimating the scope of the project. Due to a lack of experience, the biggest challenge was not being realistic about the complexity of the project. Instead of being transparent, the engineers and designers started cutting corners and rushing the schedule, which only exacerbated the problems.

It's common to make the same mistakes the City of Boston made. When you misunderstand a project's scope and needs, you are likely to create an unrealistic timeline, and failure to meet deadlines is almost guaranteed.

That's because estimating is difficult—and the further out in time one estimates, the more imprecise the estimate will be. Do the complete opposite. Focus less on the bird's-eye view of the entire project, break it down into individual tasks, and study them in detail.

Keep in mind that good timelines require real honesty. What can you really accomplish? The only way to answer that accurately is to take your project down to the incremental level. Then, when you think about the project's overall timeline, you'll be able to make a more confident estimate, not a guesstimate.

KEY TAKEAWAYS

✓ Get feedback from your team on what can reasonably be achieved.

✓ Be practical, and train yourself to think in smaller increments so you'll be successful and on time.

✓ Be transparent about what you can get done. Track what you've done and use that experience in a retrospective meeting to help you improve.

THE DOWNSIDE OF MULTITASKING

Many agree that Leonardo da Vinci is the perfect example of a Renaissance man—a person with talents in many disciplines, from painting and sculpture to architecture, science, mechanics, and war. But he's also known for never finishing his work. At his death in 1519, Leonardo left many of his greatest paintings incomplete, and he never actually built out any of the blueprints that filled his journals.

Leonardo's situation highlights one of the biggest risks of multitasking. Because no single task ever receives full attention, the chances are greater that many will be left incomplete. That hasn't gotten in the way of Leonardo's reputation as a genius, but the rest of us aren't so lucky. The fact is, multitasking isn't a time-saver—it actually reduces productivity and leads to mistakes and underperformance.

Teams tend to drift and miss key milestones and metrics when they spread themselves too thin. Limit tasks in order to keep on track. Reject a multitasking approach and opt for tackling each task one at a time. When team members concentrate on a single task, they finish sooner and produce information that usually helps with other tasks in the iteration.

When devoting energies to finishing a single task, you can give results to stakeholders sooner. That builds their confidence in your team's abilities and often quickens the team's pace. It will more than likely allow you to complete your project sooner than projected.

KEY TAKEAWAYS

- ✓ Don't take on another task until the current one is done, unless you're waiting for other team members.
- ✓ Set expectations and communicate that a new task won't be started until the current one is finished.
- ✓ Remember that multitasking is distracting and affects your ability to correctly understand your team's productivity.

KEEP YOUR EYE ON ONE BALL

Bill Gates once said, "My success, part of it certainly, is that I have focused in on a few things."[16] Gates and Paul Allen had a vision that every home would have a personal computer. At the time, it was a concept that seemed unfathomable. In order to accomplish such a feat, Allen said that Gates would focus on one task at a time with extreme discipline.

Stakeholders can sometimes feel like serious obstacles when striving to meet your goals and achieve the many objectives for your project. As a project manager, it's your job to support your stakeholders' business requirements. But it's a tough balancing act when stakeholders feel the need to change their priorities, and in turn, yours. Preempt your stakeholders' concerns and manage their expectations by keeping them updated on the project's progress vis-à-vis objectives.

Stakeholders' concerns about a project's perceived lack of progress or wrong direction may compel them to intervene. How can you optimize your team's effectiveness when your stakeholders are tempted to control how the work is done?

Build stakeholder trust by prioritizing your tasks in alignment with their objectives. Keep stakeholders apprised of the plan, share progress, and show accomplishments so they see how well the team is meeting their needs.

KEY TAKEAWAYS

- ✓ Advise stakeholders of your team's need to focus on one prioritized activity at a time.
- ✓ Stay disciplined. Minimize distractions and encourage team members to focus on one task at a time.
- ✓ Align your team's priorities on stakeholder objectives.
- ✓ Reassure stakeholders by sharing progress and showing accomplishments.

TARGET PRACTICE

Genghis Khan was the ultimate conqueror, founding, then expanding, the largest land empire the world has ever seen. During his rise to power, he recruited many trusted associates—sometimes by unconventional means. There are some variations to the story, but one narrative holds that in 1201, an enemy warrior named Jirqo'adai shot and killed Khan's horse.[17] After the enemy surrendered, Khan demanded to know who shot the arrow, and Jirqo'adai boldly took credit. Khan decided to reward his audacity by making him a powerful companion and giving him the new name of *Jebe,* which translates as "arrow" or "weapon."

Stakeholders rarely have only one project in motion, and they're likely to be in a constant state of project analysis as factors change. The best way to stay off their radar is by putting yourself *on* their radar with results that are responsive to these changes. Vested stakeholders often continually analyze and evaluate your team's productivity and progress against moving targets. If this is not handled well, you might spend more time responding to their concerns than managing your project.

Hone your aim on project targets by continuous reflection and adjust when efforts don't go well. Regular, positive, and responsive progress reports foster satisfied stakeholders and empower your team to build on their successes. By working in small task iterations, your team can show results faster, minimize productivity lost due to wrong turns, and increase the quality of their work. This leads to higher productivity for your team and, ultimately, the whole organization.

By establishing clearly defined goals and building the necessary road-map, teams can adjust and be reminded of their intended objectives. Although your objectives might change, you must always understand where the target is.

KEY TAKEAWAYS

✓ Establish clear goals and objectives.

✓ Reevaluate objectives in a controlled, organized process.

✓ Communicate with your stakeholders and make sure they are aware that you are focused on their priorities.

BE READY FOR THE UNEXPECTED

One of the most anticipated moments in movie history took place at the end of 1983's *Return of the Jedi*—the unmasking of Darth Vader. Moviegoers didn't know what to expect, and Luke Skywalker didn't either. That epic unveiling was the chance to finally see the tragic human being hiding behind one of the most fearsome masks in the galaxy. But when the mask was finally taken away, there was no sinister-looking monster staring back. As both mythologist Joseph Campbell and series creator George Lucas agreed, Vader was nothing but a weak, inhuman flunky.[18,19] Audiences were stunned.

Movies often rely on such shocking and unexpected moments. In project management, however, no team ever wants to reach the end of a project and experience that kind of deflating shock. To avoid surprises, teams have to do the seemingly impossible: prepare for the unexpected. How? Because project outcomes usually evolve, the best teams are the ones that put a high value on flexibility and adaptation. They understand that planning for unanticipated changes isn't a waste of time—it's a realistic (and necessary) part of the project process to discuss your response to every "what if" scenario.

Bring together the team—along with key stakeholders—to brainstorm potential risks and changes. Start this conversation early in the process and do it throughout the project. Periodic reassessments are necessary whenever conditions change. It's the best way to stay on the right course, and your stakeholders will appreciate it.

KEY TAKEAWAYS

- ✓ Anticipate potential changes that might lie ahead, and be ready to adapt as needed.
- ✓ Reassess throughout the project to identify potential issues before it's too late.
- ✓ Preparation for change improves the team's readiness for it and ensures a better result for the project.

COACH THE TEAM THROUGH CHANGE

According to the World Health Organization, a pandemic is "the world-wide spread of a new disease."[20] In March 2020, COVID-19 was declared a pandemic, and everyday life changed dramatically for people around the world.

Change impacts lives, daily norms, and levels of comfort, and it invites resistance. As a project manager, you are a leader, and you have great influence over how to manage change with systems and iterations. Yet when it comes to a team, the human element makes things trickier. Be flexible and view change as an opportunity, not an obstacle.

Disruptions are common in the business world, and significant ones can drastically alter the strategies and mission of any organization or team. If change becomes problematic and painful due to resistance from team members, how you frame change is critical. Consider what changes might occur during the course of a project. Then, be proactive about how you'll adapt to those changes. This practice will help the team develop the skills and qualities needed to adapt and respond, avoiding failure and reducing the risk of future disasters.

The more you allow flexibility in your thinking about change—considering it as a tool to generate opportunities—the more you minimize your team's fear of and negative response to it. Give team members a chance to develop problem-solving skills and to experiment, innovate, and find new ways around disruptions together. Let your team experience success and learn that change is an opportunity.

KEY TAKEAWAYS

✓ Discuss how your team will respond to change.

✓ Allow your team to experiment and innovate together, and don't dwell on mistakes.

✓ Acknowledge successes and disappointments and use each as an opportunity to learn.

✓ Anticipate and accept criticism, then work with it and learn how to successfully respond.

EVEN SMALL LOSSES ADD UP

Six thousand dollars. That's how much loose change an average American loses in their lifetime according to tracking experts—the equivalent of two first class round trip plane tickets to Italy or a nice summer getaway for the entire family![21] It's hard to appreciate the overall amount when you're only thinking of the dime that fell out of your pocket on the taxi ride home.

What happens to the average American happens to businesses every day when they don't think ahead in terms of preparing for and running meetings. Wasted minutes add up like lost loose change and affect everything—deadlines, performance, productivity, and, in the long run, how your client feels about working with you.

Without specific goals and objectives, conversations, questions, and other incidental distractions can rapidly take your projects off course. Meeting agendas are the project manager's most effective tool to keep teams focused on a project's purpose and objectives. Stay focused. Use a timebox (a fixed time period for a planned activity) approach to ensure that every item is covered in the allotted time. You don't want meetings to go off on a tangent.

A list of bullet points isn't enough to keep a meeting on course. Prep work and a simplified focus are the keys to ensuring a productive meeting in the time prescribed. Have an agenda for every meeting and establish boundaries. Set time limits to help you and your team stay on track and keep your project moving forward.

KEY TAKEAWAYS

✓ Identify specific goals and outcomes for each meeting with a detailed agenda.

✓ Communicate the agenda and objectives of the meeting in advance to allow participants to prepare and coordinate their other activities.

✓ Set defined periods of time for each item on the agenda to avoid detours.

✓ Start the meeting on time and plan for meetings to conclude ten minutes ahead of schedule.

CASE STUDY

SUMMARY

Juggling too many responsibilities at once is not productive. In addition to being distracting, it can reduce your productivity level and wreak havoc on your time management. That said, there are times when you may have to juggle a variety of tasks related to a project (or several), but it's wise to be selective about what you take on. It's best to achieve one task or finish one project at a time whenever possible to minimize juggling.

PROBLEM

When T2 was engaged by a client to support the acquisition and IT transition of the client's health system, the number of projects that had to be completed in a short period of time was overwhelming. It was difficult to make much progress because each department group, as well as attendant third parties, all wanted information at the same time. This amount of juggling was unproductive and ineffective.

SOLUTION

T2 took a step back and created a list of all the client's projects. We then assessed each project's priority, determining what was most critical to the organization. Once we were able to reset the expectations of the stakeholders and various departments, T2 was able to focus its resources on one or two projects at a time. This enabled us to work productively to complete the high-priority items and then move on to the next project. Working in this focused manner allowed us to quickly address the highest priority items and ultimately complete all of the projects more quickly than we would have had we worked on all of them at once.

JUGGLING

EMPOWERMENT

Empowering your team members means that instead of **dictating** how things will be done, you encourage them to take action and make decisions within your organization—particularly, during the course of a project. It signals that there is trust and understanding in place and that you know they are working to accomplish goals and satisfy stakeholders as well as one another.

Using a **"pull, don't push" approach** gives your team the power to act as its own arbiter and its members to challenge one another to excel. Often the result is an overall sense of deep accomplishment and an uptick in the productivity of the group. For such an outcome to occur, project managers must promote a sense of team unity and harmony. The **strength of your team** is greater than the sum of its individual parts. Leverage the skills of each team member, but take responsibility as a single unit for all of your actions.

As a project manager, it's in your best interest to motivate team members to learn, grow, and experience **failure** on their way to success. When they are ready to **spread their wings,** you too will benefit from their independence.

When teams **work together** well, members not only become more committed to the project, they become more committed to one another. Every team member must be engaged because **all it takes is one** who is not to diminish the success of the project. Don't assign all the important tasks to just a few team members. Rotate responsibilities to allow various members of the team to shine in key areas. **Applaud helping hands,** and encourage star performers to mentor other members of the team. Developing new talent enhances long-term productivity, and **the show must go on.**

A key factor in empowering team members is to provide an environment where they can speak freely and constructively and feel respected. Establish ground rules that, to further collaboration, team members will keep their **egos in check** and not take anything personally.

Give your team a **confidence boost** now and then by creating opportunities for them to achieve and celebrate smaller goals. Understand their capabilities and **find the right pace.** The key is to locate the balance between productivity and momentum that works best for you and integrate that knowledge into your team.

Empowering your team is as much about attitude and mindset as it is about specific tools and processes. It's based on positive interactions and a spirit of camaraderie, so always remember to **accentuate the positive!**

DON'T DICTATE, INNOVATE!

Considering he held 1,093 patents in his lifetime—a record-setting number—it's no wonder Thomas Edison is regarded as the embodiment of invention. While undoubtedly a genius, what made him so remarkable was not just what he accomplished, but also how he worked. His Menlo Park laboratory, where teams of scientists and workers were free to collaborate and experiment to develop remarkable products, was arguably the world's first research and development facility for general invention.

Edison didn't dictate solutions from the top down but rather encouraged innovation to solve problems and improve outcomes. He realized that when you tell people what to do or think about a project, you're killing the chances that they'll come up with innovative solutions and reducing their investment in the outcome.

Encourage others to brainstorm and produce solutions together rather than dictate how to solve a problem or tackle a project. Not only will this produce better products, plans, or services, it will also lead to a greater sense of accountability for everyone, reinforcing team cohesion and increasing self-motivation for all.

When you tell people what to do or think about a project, you're killing the chances that they'll innovate, and you reduce their investment in it.

KEY TAKEAWAYS

- ✓ Avoid dictating how best to approach a problem. Instead, ask each team member to offer solutions.
- ✓ Empower team members to think outside the box and discover solutions on their own. This will lead to greater individual and team accountability.
- ✓ Encourage your team to believe they can make a difference so they will share their ideas.
- ✓ Foster team success to help motivate team members to be more innovative.

PULL, DON'T PUSH

During his legendary career, Walt Disney adopted many leadership styles. He kept a firm grip on what he wanted, whether it was a new animated movie or a theme park ride. But Disney also knew that taking a too authoritarian approach would smother the creativity of his artists.

Instead, when it came to planning animation, he'd describe his overall vision and then let his legion of artists use their own skills and perspectives to achieve it. While the goal was firmly set, the way to get there was left up to them. At the time, Disney's approach was referred to as "participatory leadership." It's also a version of the "pull" methodology that's popular today.

The "pull" approach lets teams organize and regulate themselves to maximize productivity and momentum. It's more effective than the traditional "push" approach, which imposes rules, timelines, procedures, and methods with no consideration of a team's actual abilities or the validity of the goal. The best creative situations occur when team members get "pulled," not "pushed," to uncover their own unique contributions to a team's performance.

The "push" versus "pull" debate requires a delicate balance to be struck. In most situations, a "pull" approach centering on the team works best for optimal results, but sometimes a nudge may be required. The highest performing businesses tap into the creative and collaborative abilities of teams and, at the same time, recognize the need for authority when hard decisions need to be made.

KEY TAKEAWAYS

- ✓ Use the "pull" approach to lead instead of the policing and micromanaging methods of the "push" approach.
- ✓ Ask, don't dictate: your team will be more fully engaged with the project at hand.
- ✓ Rather than set timelines without consensus, let the team establish what its capabilities are.

STRENGTH IN NUMBERS

In one of Aesop's fables, a father couldn't convince his sons to stop quarreling. He decided to make his point another way. Presenting his sons with a bundle of sticks, he challenged them to break the bundle—and not one of them could do it. When the father asked his sons to separate the bundle and break the sticks one at a time, they did so easily.

The father showed his sons that there is strength in unity. Together, like a bundle of sticks, a group can be unbreakable. For the project manager, there's a similar takeaway: your team will be stronger and able to achieve far better outcomes when you leverage the skills of the whole team, rather than just those of a few participants.

Seek input from everyone on your team and empower them to use their talents and experience collectively. Team members will be more likely to engage with one another and the project in productive ways as a result. Working as a whole, they are more likely to feel invested and be willing to take responsibility than when they fear being singled out.

Encourage team unity and harmony. The strength of your team is greater than the sum of its individual parts. Collaborate as individuals, but take responsibility as a single unit for all of your actions. By empowering your team to become self-sufficient and share responsibility for failures as well as successes, they will gain a large measure of confidence that will positively affect every project they undertake.

KEY TAKEAWAYS

✓ Leverage the skills of your whole team for better outcomes.

✓ Encourage all members of your team to contribute their unique skills and insights to a project.

✓ Foster a collaborative environment in which offering ideas and feedback is valued and appreciated.

✓ Work as a single team, committing to and taking responsibility for one another's actions.

✓ Coach your team to rely on one another.

WITH FAILURE COMES SUCCESS

When basketball superstar Michael Jordan was in tenth grade, he tried out for the varsity team and didn't make it. He was so devastated that he went home, shut the door to his bedroom, and cried. Failure, though, fired up his desire to improve, and the next year he made varsity—and five years after that, he was in the NBA.

The story doesn't end there. Jordan may have become one of the NBA's greatest players, but he also had plenty of failures. During his NBA career, he missed over twelve thousand shots and lost more than three hundred games. "I've failed over and over again in my life," he said in a famous commercial, "and that is why I succeed." As noble as this sounds, in the business world, too many managers are reluctant to let their teams have the kind of learning experience that Jordan did, despite how beneficial this can be for a team.

The fact is, some bosses rule with a heavy hand and get great results—in the short run. That heavy hand also conditions their team to be overly dependent on them. When these bosses are absent, their teams don't know what to do or how to make any decisions. You will always get more from people who have learned from their own failures, like Jordan, than from those who just did what their bosses wanted.

Managers and other stakeholders must restrain the micromanaging impulse and the fear that things won't get done well without them. Using open-ended questions is a good way to shift into a coaching role. Such questions empower team members to exercise their problem-solving abilities even at the risk of failing.

KEY TAKEAWAYS

✓ Balance project goals with allowing your team to discover its skills.

✓ Coach your team with open-ended questions that provoke and encourage independent thinking.

✓ Allow for failure and coach team members through their mistakes.

✓ Avoid a top-down leadership approach because it leaves the team too dependent.

✓ Aim to make your team self-sufficient in the long run.

WHEN TEAM MEMBERS SPREAD THEIR WINGS

Naturalists say that mother birds use food to coax their babies out of the nest and encourage them to fly. These mothers stand farther and farther out on a branch with the food, even though that means the baby bird will fall. Repeated falls eventually teach the babies to flap their wings to break their fall and return to the branch for their next meal.

It's a repetitive process that instills the independence birds need to survive on their own. This approach to learning isn't unique to the animal kingdom: it happens in work environments, too. Often teams are composed of members with varying levels of experience: some are seasoned, while others are more recent arrivals to the workforce. This is a useful dynamic that many project managers overlook.

Every project presents an opportunity for growth and for project managers to shift into a coaching role. When project managers become coaches instead of bosses, they help their teams to become more self-sufficient and learn to move tasks forward on their own.

Coaching and teaching self-sufficiency have a powerful reciprocal effect. When a team learns to become more independent, the project manager has more time to focus on identifying and resolving future issues.

KEY TAKEAWAYS

✓ Ask open-ended questions so your team solves problems on their own.

✓ Change the top-down dynamic that says only the manager has the answers.

✓ Encourage your team to be open to new ideas and perspectives.

✓ Allow your team to talk freely and openly so that new ideas will flow.

THE TEAM THAT WORKS TOGETHER

One of the greatest examples of team cooperation comes not from management books but from the world of film. Akira Kurosawa's epic 1954 movie *Seven Samurai* shows the power—and effect—of team cohesion when seven warriors unite to defend a farming village against an army of bandits.

It might seem like the bandits have an unfair advantage because their numbers are greater, but when the warriors work together, understanding one another's strengths and weaknesses and thinking of creative ways to defend the village, their power is multiplied exponentially. This concept is articulated in the Agile philosophy: when teams work well together, their cohesiveness translates into greater effectiveness.

Some teams cringe at learning together on the job and prefer to have a complete plan and rigid expectations instead. That's a mistake. The Agile philosophy recognizes that project goals can change with every iteration, and a well-coordinated team should be able to adapt to these changes so results reflect the current situation, not what it was six months ago when the project started.

Teams that don't work together and take responsibility for their performance won't learn how to work independently and respond to project challenges. Every project offers a chance for teams to learn how to collaborate effectively and succeed. When that happens, team members not only become more committed to the project—they also become more committed to one another.

KEY TAKEAWAYS

✓ Treat every project as an opportunity to have your team learn the value of cohesion and accountability.

✓ Give teams members a chance to problem solve and learn from one another.

✓ Develop a healthy dynamic of cooperation among team members.

ALL IT TAKES IS ONE

When it comes to unusual feats of human ingenuity, "Domino Day" in the Netherlands was a ten-plus-year tradition that took those familiar game pieces and created incredibly intricate patterns of falling tiles that would impress any engineer. From 1998 to 2009, each successive "Domino Day" outdid the last one with new patterns and challenges—not to mention hundreds of thousands more tiles. Each new contest brought another new world record.[22]

That all came to an end in 2007 when a pattern that included a moving bridge of dominoes failed to fall—and 400,000 dominoes were left standing.[23] The lesson? All it takes is one. What happened at the 2007 "Domino Day" can happen to any team. Just a single team member who isn't fully engaged—like one poorly placed domino—can have a significant effect on the project's outcome.

Teams function best when every member is engaged. There are a variety of reasons why some might not be—they may feel intimidated or not fully invested in what's at stake, for example—but it's critical to find ways to draw them out so that everyone is involved.

Empower each team member so that they become accountable. This will keep every member more engaged, focused, and committed to helping the team to succeed.

KEY TAKEAWAYS

- ✓ Identify the skills of non-contributing team members and find alternate ways to involve them.
- ✓ Make your team accountable to one another in order to establish a cohesive effort.
- ✓ Discuss with your team how each person's input is important to the project.
- ✓ Reiterate a team commitment to group responsibility for performance and results.

APPLAUD HELPING HANDS

When parents peek inside a Montessori classroom, they see an interesting dynamic at work: students of multiple ages, helping one another. It's a far cry from the traditional classrooms that most people remember from childhood.

That's because Maria Montessori believed in creating an environment that reflects the real world and encourages students to discover their talents. That includes learning the value of helping (and receiving help from) other students who are younger, the same age, or older than they are. Learning to teach one another is not just a powerful lesson found in Montessori classrooms: the best teams believe in it, too.

Most people struggle with asking for help because it's considered a sign of weakness. But when the good of the team is at stake, asking for help isn't a weakness—failing to ask for it is. Teams thrive when members pitch in and assist colleagues who are struggling or feeling overwhelmed. When team members witness how people can learn from one another, it's a powerful experience that strengthens the team.

There's nothing more valuable in a team setting than encouraging members to ask for help and teach one another. The assistance benefits not just the team member receiving it but the whole team. Stepping out of one's comfort zone to help someone else fosters selflessness and contributes to the team's overall performance.

KEY TAKEAWAYS

✓ Create a culture of cooperation that values giving and receiving help.

✓ Don't hide your problems from your team. Sooner or later, they will come out.

✓ Communicate early and often to your team to offer or ask for help when it's needed.

✓ Keep up team momentum by asking a knowledgeable colleague to help another who is having problems.

THE SHOW MUST GO ON

When legendary actor Laurence Olivier had to undergo treatment for prostate cancer in 1967 during his run in a play, he had no choice: he had to rely on his understudy to take his place.

Olivier's replacement was a nervous young actor named Anthony Hopkins. Even though this was many years before *The Silence of the Lambs* and his other hits, Hopkins easily filled the older actor's shoes and enjoyed great success with the Royal National Theatre before becoming a movie star. Understudies who can play the main roles are crucial in theater. The same is true in any team, and it's important to have several members who are good at the same task.

When workloads aren't spread evenly across your team, productivity and efficiency are bound to suffer, and your star performers will too. Burnout is inevitable. It's also unfair to deprive other members of the chance to learn a particular task just because key employees are better at it. Find ways to tap into those specialized skills to develop and enhance the rest of the team.

Don't concentrate important tasks on only a few members of the team. Instead, leverage their specialized expertise so that everyone learns. In the long run, this will boost your team's sense of self-esteem and overall success.

KEY TAKEAWAYS

✓ Distribute tasks among the entire team, not just those with specialized skills.

✓ Enhance long-term productivity by having star performers mentor their colleagues.

✓ Reduce performance risk by collaborating and sharing knowledge.

✓ Rotate responsibilities to allow others the opportunity to shine in key areas.

KEEP YOUR EGO IN CHECK

When billionaire investor Warren Buffett bought the now one-hundred-year-old retailer Helzberg Diamonds in 1995, he followed a simple rule: stay out of the way. Buffett resisted doing what many investors do after making an acquisition—that is, stepping in and making changes, even when they might be necessary.

Instead he simply marveled at the retailer's success and recognized the talented people running the show, and he chose not to interfere. Barnett Helzberg, the previous owner of the company, was so impressed by Buffett's behavior that he wrote the book *What I Learned Before I Sold to Warren Buffett*. When you take your ego out of the picture, Helzberg writes, better decisions get made because everyone focuses on what is best for the company. "Egoless management," he explains, "can be your greatest strength."[24]

In a team setting, entering a planning session with an egoless attitude is vital because every project and iteration is different and brings its own challenges and dilemmas. It's tempting to cut corners here and seek an easy fix by drawing on past experiences or get defensive when other people question your ideas. But it also limits your ability to innovate and look ahead. Instead, encourage team members to be open-minded and reserve judgment.

From the start, be transparent with your team and establish, as a ground rule, that no one should take anything personally. Strive for integrity and excellence and remember that the key to your team's success is fostered by the mindset you all share.

KEY TAKEAWAYS

✓ During planning sessions, encourage team members to embrace their identity as a team and recognize that each person has a role.

✓ Begin each iteration by reminding team members to respect one another and begin with a clean mental slate.

✓ Talk about what the team is doing, not what individuals have done.

✓ Make room for every person's ideas so that they realize they are all in the project together.

✓ Establish that all victories are earned by the entire team.

FIND THE RIGHT PACE AND DON'T LOSE IT

For a marathoner, discovering the pace that works best and sticking to it is everything. World record holder Haile Gebrselassie learned this the hard way. In 2007, the Ethiopian runner wowed the world at the Berlin Marathon when he became the first person to run a marathon in under two hours and four and a half minutes. The next year, in Dubai, fans eagerly expected him to break that record.

Gebrselassie seemed well on his way. By the race's halfway mark, he was running sixty-one seconds faster than he had in his record-breaking marathon in Berlin. But because he increased his pace so much, he faded badly in the race's last miles, and he finished twenty-eight seconds slower than his record. This is a cautionary tale for any team member. Being successful requires knowing your work rate and productivity levels. It's important to know your limits, not just your strengths.

Why? Because this knowledge teaches you to pace yourself accordingly, something that Gebrselassie seemed to forget in Dubai. Go too fast, and you will struggle at the end. Go too slow, and you won't see the finish line. The key is to find the balance between productivity and momentum that works best for you.

Be honest about your abilities. The practice of being successful requires a good understanding of your abilities and what you can honestly commit to. Team members thrive—and the team does too—when they know their performance limits and exercise good self-discipline on tasks.

KEY TAKEAWAYS

✓ Learn to win by understanding your team's strengths and limits.

✓ Help team members develop a sense of intuitiveness and self-discipline that fits into the overall work of the team.

✓ Encourage each team member to think through their commitments and understand the work rhythm that's right for them.

✓ Learn with your team what their work rate is by reflecting on past performance levels.

ACCENTUATE THE POSITIVE

As the world struggled to rebuild after World War II, a New York City minister wanted to do his part. His solution was a system of simple principles for better living that eventually became the book *The Power of Positive Thinking*. The minister, Norman Vincent Peale, published the book in 1952, and it became a runaway bestseller that has sold at least fifteen million copies worldwide.

The most common cause of people's troubles, Peale said, was negative thinking. He asked readers to apply a positive outlook to every area of their lives, from family relationships to office behavior. For him, every mistake was a chance to improve and every person (even the rude ones) deserved the benefit of the doubt. The team approach to project management is built on the same ideas that made Peale a bestselling author.

But what's also true for teams is what Peale's critics often said: staying positive is a nice idea, but it's much harder to put into practice. It's easier to see the negative in situations and people, especially if you disagree with the way someone handles a situation. But everyone makes mistakes and deserves another chance. The sooner you realize and accept that, the better it will be for you and your team.

The team approach is as much about attitude and mindset as it is about specific tools and processes. It's based on positive interactions and camaraderie. It's important for you and the members of your team to practice positivity in every aspect of the business, whether in interactions with a stakeholder or with one another.

KEY TAKEAWAYS

✓ Promote a culture in which people's faults are not unduly magnified and mistakes are not pointed out to punish colleagues.

✓ Encourage your team more often and dwell on problems less.

✓ Treat faults and mistakes as actionable items that can ultimately benefit the team.

✓ Even if you dislike how something is handled, do your best to understand the situation.

CASE STUDY

SUMMARY

Empowering your team means recognizing that each member has value and can contribute to the project, and this enhances productivity and overall excellence. It also encourages team members to be self-sufficient so they are not too dependent on others. To empower them, you, as the project manager, must lead with gentle guidance that allows team members to learn from their mistakes and discover how to better interact with one another.

PROBLEM

A client asked T2 to do an assessment of what was needed to bring the client's newly acquired hospital up to the parent company's IT standards within sixty days. This required T2 to establish multiple teams to cover all the IT disciplines working with the staff at the parent company, third-party vendors, and the current managed-service providers. The goal was to produce a project plan and estimate the cost to integrate the hospital into the parent company in a very short period of time.

SOLUTION

T2 created multiple teams and clearly outlined each team's objectives, allowing each team to be accountable for developing the assessment for its respective discipline. Each team was in charge of allocating responsibilities, estimating how long the task would take, and determining how they would achieve the expected result. This approach reduced the need for oversight since each team was empowered and held accountable. Using this approach, T2 was able to complete the project in the requested sixty days.

COMMUNICATION

Communicating clearly and effectively is at the root of almost every human interaction. It certainly is the bedrock of project management, as it is with any business endeavor.

Before team leaders embark on a project, it's crucial to identify the stakeholders with whom the team will be communicating. Stakeholders exist at many levels within an organization, and the key is to seek out and forge alliances with the ones who have the **power to make decisions** regarding your project. To do that, you should first find them, **understand their expectations,** and then keep them updated with information that addresses their needs. However, **don't overdo it.** Avoid treating every issue as if it is an emergency.

When it comes to communications with your team, the more the better. Clarity is essential to project success, so be sure to fully organize your thoughts and focus on how to accomplish the work. **Don't create an avalanche** by letting problems build. To **keep the team synchronized,** share the same level of information with all team members and use visual tools to track progress and each member's role in it.

Transparency in your communications will build **trusting,** productive working relationships between all parties involved in the project. **Answer questions promptly** and directly. **Grow thicker skin** and remember to **control your emotions**. When emotions take over, professionalism is lost. **Read between your lines** to remove the potential for misinterpretation.

Most importantly, make sure that your messages are received. Passive forms of communication, such as email and voicemail, place the burden of responsibility on the sender. So, if your **email goes unanswered**, take the necessary steps to confirm that it made its way to its intended recipient.

Last of all, consider when to communicate. Be mindful that measured silence can speak volumes. **Knowing when to speak up** and when not to is an acquired trait well worth cultivating.

TAP INTO STAKEHOLDER POWER

In *The Empire Strikes Back*, Yoda said that "only a fully trained Jedi Knight, with the Force as his ally, will conquer Vader and his Emperor."

While your projects don't have to contend with Darth Vader or the Emperor, finding the right allies makes a galaxy of difference when it comes to ensuring a project's success.

Stakeholders exist at many levels within an organization. They may be directly involved with your project, or merely affected by its activities or outcome. The key is to actively seek out and forge alliances with the ones who are respected, influential, and have the authority to make decisions. But how do you engage stakeholders when they have multiple priorities and you need their support?

Convert your stakeholders into true believers. Do this by providing them with regular information, showing team success, incorporating their input into the project objectives, involving them in solving road-blocks encountered by the team, and building the trust needed for them to empower you.

KEY TAKEAWAYS

✓ Identify stakeholders who have the authority to make decisions.

✓ Get to know your stakeholders' perspective(s) and learn about their vision and challenges.

✓ Build trust by sharing your team's successes and challenges.

✓ Keep stakeholders informed with information targeted to address their needs.

UNDERSTAND YOUR STAKEHOLDER

"Get up front!" When his officers needed to tell him something, that's what legendary General George S. Patton wanted them to do.[25] He wanted direct, simple engagement from his subordinates with no hesitation. He didn't want anyone to waste his time, Porter Williamson, one of his former staff officers, explained—and Patton's officers were certainly never in any doubt about what the general wanted.

Williamson and his fellow officers knew Patton so well that he influenced every aspect of their military careers. "No man served under Gen. Patton," Williamson wrote in his memoir. "He was always serving with us. In truth, I still serve with Gen. Patton, and he continues to serve with me."[26] Though it isn't necessary to get to that depth of understanding with your stakeholders, it *is* necessary to have a very clear picture of what they want and to provide them with exactly what they need.

To be successful, provide stakeholders with accurate data about project deliverables and progress. Refine and focus the information you have as much as possible. Don't waffle or waste their time. Give them solid facts and clearly articulated metrics so they understand your team's situation and how it aligns with the project's charter. Treat sponsor updates like you would an elevator pitch: brief, informative, and to the point.

Reports or presentations for your project's stakeholders should demonstrate in a clear way what your team has accomplished. If the project involves something concrete—for example, creating a piece of software or print materials—put a sample in their hands. Make your team's success tangible to stakeholders and let them witness it for themselves. This will increase their trust.

KEY TAKEAWAYS

✓ Be on point when providing progress updates to your stakeholders.

✓ Demonstrate and engage the stakeholders not only about problems, but also about what the team accomplished.

✓ Provide a realistic picture of where the project is, ideally via concrete examples.

✓ Engage stakeholders to help provide clarity on project priorities and direction.

INFORM STAKEHOLDERS, BUT DON'T OVERDO IT

Technology has changed many things about modern life, but it hasn't replaced one of the most indispensable roles in the US Army: the cavalry scout. Scouts weren't just the eyes and ears of US forces on the frontier in the mid-nineteenth century—they're still critical today. In a combat situation, these soldiers forge ahead of the troops and gather critical information on enemy positions and movements.

When it comes to important stakeholders, your team functions much like a cavalry scout. You're the one with up-to-the-minute intel on a project's momentum and any evolving challenges that are valuable to stakeholders. Make sure to report this information to stakeholders at the end of every iteration—don't delay. Imagine if military scouts weren't prompt: the outcome could be disastrous.

Give periodic updates after—but not during—every iteration. Don't break the cadence unless there's an absolute emergency and you have no choice. Take a lesson from these scouts and get comfortable with the fact that stakeholders need regular reports even when there's nothing significant to say. Knowing that an iteration went as planned is sometimes just what they need to hear.

Effective teams provide helpful information to stakeholders with decision-making authority that can affect their efforts. Keep your communications with your stakeholder to a regular cadence unless it is very urgent. When your team treats every issue as urgent, it becomes increasingly difficult for stakeholders to know when something is a real emergency.

KEY TAKEAWAYS

✓ Provide stakeholders with regular updates, even if everything is going as planned.

✓ Present planned team accomplishments as a part of the update process.

✓ Report what your team completed after each iteration.

✓ Don't treat every issue as urgent and try not break your planned cadence.

DON'T CREATE AN AVALANCHE

The startup Quirky was founded in 2009 and raised a whopping 185 million dollars in venture capital.[27] Three years later it was filing for bankruptcy protection. The company was purchased in 2015 for 4.7 million dollars and relaunched in 2017.[28, 29] Quirky's failure lay in bringing to market too many products too soon. Instead of having two or three good products, Quirky rushed to develop as many products as they could, resulting in a glut of mediocre, untested gadgets that ultimately flopped.

Work piles up as more demands are thrown at you. Something's got to give, and too often the consequences are a deadline missed, poor quality work, or a project cycle falling short of its original objectives.

It's a project manager's job to make sure teams are not overwhelmed and to ensure that team members are not left to decide on their own what is most important. Project managers must clearly communicate to their team the sequence and order of priorities, based on business needs set by the stakeholders, as well as the consequences of any changes. You need to remind the team that they do not have the authority to change the priorities unless an agreement is reached with the stakeholder.

Typically, a business requires that a new project be started immediately with deadlines following soon thereafter. However, what do you do if your team is already committed and you don't have the capacity to take on new work?

The business decision defines the priority. You can only do what you can do, which includes fulfilling your responsibility to clearly communicate stakeholder decisions to your team. In addition, you need to set reasonable expectations for your stakeholders.

KEY TAKEAWAYS

✓ Understand your team's work rate and be transparent about it.

✓ Don't let problems build up by not communicating them expediently.

✓ Stay on course until you have clearly communicated the effect
of any changes.

✓ Set expectations for the consequence of new priorities or scope changes.

✓ Remember that the business and the stakeholders determine priorities,
not the team.

SYNCHRONIZE THE TEAM

At the 1936 Olympics in Berlin, a University of Washington rowing team did the unthinkable: they beat the better equipped and physically stronger German and Italian teams to win the gold. Brute strength wasn't the key, writes Daniel James Brown in *The Boys in the Boat*. It was laser-sharp communication and coordination that made the real difference.

As Brown puts it:

> The demands of rowing are such that every man or woman in a racing shell depends on his or her crewmates to perform almost flawlessly with each and every pull of the oar. The movements of each rower are so intimately intertwined, so precisely synchronized with the movements of all the others, that any one rower's mistake or subpar performance can throw off the tempo of the stroke, the balance of the boat, and ultimately the success of the whole crew.[30]

What's true for the rowers is true for you and your team members too. Your team must achieve the same level of communication and coordination as those rowers, and you must keep everyone in sync. Sometimes excluding people comes with the best intentions. Why overwhelm everyone with a group email that doesn't apply to their specific tasks? Fair question, but the answer should be obvious: you're all in the same boat.

Excluding some members from communications runs the risk of creating conflicts and interpersonal issues. Avoid offending any team member and creating potential rancor by including everyone in communications from the very beginning.

KEY TAKEAWAYS

✓ Don't decide what people should know: share the same level of information with the entire team.

✓ Maintain transparency at every stage of the project.

✓ Make everyone accountable to one another.

✓ Encourage the team to collaborate and come to a consensus on decisions.

VISUALIZE TEAM ROLES

We've all heard the aphorism: "A picture paints a thousand words." The modern use of the phrase is attributed to Fredrick R. Barnard, who wrote an article promoting the use of images in advertisements in 1921 entitled "One look is worth a thousand words."[31] Essentially, Barnard observed that graphics could tell a story as effectively as a large amount of descriptive text.

The same idea comes into play when a team uses visualization to identify who's doing what in a project. It's a quick and easy way to identify team members' roles and responsibilities without having to wade through loads of documentation. Using a map or chart with each person's role on it not only boosts accountability among members, but also sets the stage for stronger relationships.

When, for example, it's clear that some members are carrying heavier loads, the members with lighter duties can see that and offer their colleagues whatever support is needed. Maps and charts of project workloads make this possible.

Visuals are an effective way to show team members where the stress points are in the current workload. An overall map enables members to proactively help one another.

KEY TAKEAWAYS

✓ Use visual tools where possible to map the course of the project start to finish.

✓ Track team progress by using a dashboard that clearly reflects what remains to be done.

✓ Map individual team members' responsibilities to the roles that they will be expected to perform.

BUILD TRUST

As of April 2021, three million deaths have been recorded due to the COVID-19 pandemic.[32] Had China been more transparent at the start of the crisis, had many countries communicated more effectively to their citizens, and had the World Health Organization provided more timely information, it is likely fewer people would have died. In America, public trust in the CDC and the FDA is at one of its lowest points in the last few decades.[33] This comes on top of the country's failure to coordinate and minimize the impact that the pandemic has caused.

Throughout history, a lack of transparency between parties has led to business failures, wars, broken relationships, and more. Without transparent communication, a solid relationship is not possible simply because there are no foundations on which to build trust.

For project managers who continually interact with their team members and stakeholders, the key to instilling a trustful and productive working relationship is to maintain total transparency right from the start. Unplanned issues may put projects behind schedule. New factors may arise that affect budgets. But sharing all of this information in real time with those who need to know it is the best policy regardless of if it's good or bad news.

From the beginning, be transparent about all factors affecting the project and keep stakeholders in the loop about emerging challenges. Engage team members to proactively address challenges for which solutions can be found more rapidly through a collective effort.

KEY TAKEAWAYS

✓ Practice total transparency from the get-go because this will build stakeholder trust.

✓ Take the emotion out of your communication and adopt consistent, transparent, and open policy meetings.

✓ Maintain regular communication with stakeholders, regardless of how the project is going.

✓ Share all relevant information, both good and bad.

ANSWER THE QUESTION!

Surrounded at Bastogne during the Battle of the Bulge in December 1944, General Anthony McAuliffe and the US 101st Airborne Division received an ultimatum to surrender from the German commander, whose forces had encircled the Americans. McAuliffe read the ultimatum and dropped it on the floor. His one-word reply—"Nuts!"—became legendary in the annals of warfare for its brevity and directness.[34]

Almost everyone, when asked a question, has a tendency to discuss it before finally getting around to the answer. That can come off as patronizing, even insulting, in many cases because it implies that the questioner won't understand your answer. It's often done out of habit, but in addition to being disrespectful, it's a colossal waste of time.

When asked a question, get to the point and answer it if you know the answer! If need be, you can elaborate later. It takes tact and practice to answer questions quickly, clearly, and without undue rambling. Also, by answering promptly, you allow more questions to be asked.

Practice answering questions in a clear and succinct manner, and never presume you know what the questioner is thinking. Say "I don't know but I will get you the answer."

KEY TAKEAWAYS

✓ Answer the question first and then explain if necessary; get to the point quickly.

✓ If you don't know the answer to a question, tell the team or stakeholder you don't know.

✓ Stop talking to allow for more questions.

✓ Don't presume you know what the other person is thinking.

GROW THICKER SKIN

What is an Olympic athlete without a coach who provides feedback and direction? For Olympic gold medalist Michael Phelps, that coach is Bob Bowman. He first coached Michael at the North Baltimore Aquatic Club and later with the US Olympic Team. The knowledge possessed by a coach can help an athlete achieve success throughout their career. More importantly, how this knowledge is communicated to the athlete can determine their level of success. Practice and continuous feedback are, without a doubt, the most effective approaches to achieving Olympic-level success.

While it may be unpleasant for some, frank, professional feedback is an essential component of project management and should always be viewed in a positive way. It wouldn't be a stretch to say that it may even help rescue your project. Legitimate, constructive feedback helps you grow in your professional role, mature as an individual, and aligns you with the needs of the project and your team. It can also provide a clearer picture of what is expected from you or the project, and in turn, increase your efficiency.

Imagine the following scenario: an important stakeholder in your project has called for a meeting with you to express concerns about the project. Do you delay until you can find out what their concerns are through other channels, hoping to resolve them in advance?

No. Instead, welcome the meeting. Don't take feedback personally. Strive to see the perspective of the individual providing it. Put yourself in their shoes and seek to understand what drives their concerns. Be ready to listen openly and actively and, where appropriate, collaborate with them to identify a workable solution to their feedback.

KEY TAKEAWAYS

✓ Encourage feedback and don't take professional criticism personally.

✓ Don't be afraid to ask questions to get a better understanding of what's required.

✓ If the feedback is from a team member, welcome it and seek the truth.

✓ Sincerely thank the person for their feedback and encourage more.

CONTROL YOUR EMOTIONS

Jack Welch, former chairman and CEO of General Electric, tells a story of when he was the young manufacturing head of a plant producing a new plastic. Early on, there was an explosion that caused the roof of the plant to cave in, after which Welch was called to the home office to explain to his bosses what had happened. But instead of being harshly criticized and fired, his superiors calmly asked Welch if he knew how to fix the problem.[35]

In one afternoon, Welch learned a lesson he never forgot: by not letting emotions gain the upper hand, problems can be solved calmly, constructively, and in a professional manner. In Welch's case, the discussion with his boss turned an expensive mistake into an opportunity to learn how to correct the problem. The end result led to a better product.

Slow down and don't react too quickly. When emotions take over and drive discussions, self-control, which is the cornerstone of being a professional, is lost. To maintain control of your emotions, you can't take things personally.

It's important to think rationally and understand where you are at all times. Like a game of chess, if you can see a few moves ahead and control your desire to react too quickly, you will be better able to strategize, control how you speak, what you say, and how you will be perceived by your audience.

KEY TAKEAWAYS

✓ Don't let your emotions get the better of you. Leave them out of your professional dealings.

✓ Exercise greater emotional control for increased professionalism.

✓ Don't react too quickly—slow down and think before you speak.

READ BETWEEN YOUR LINES

During his trip to Poland in 1977, Jimmy Carter's remarks were mistranslated, leading to a politically embarrassing moment for the United States. President Carter had intended to express an interest in the Polish people's desire for their future, but the translator said that the president "desired the Poles"—sexually.

While a project manager's communications don't carry the same weight as a president's, their clarity, concision, and accuracy are of the highest priority—emails included. Otherwise, misunderstandings may arise, relationships can be damaged unintentionally, and action can become counterproductive, leading to later, remedial corrections.

Like all business professionals, project managers often find themselves under the pressure of time to communicate an important update while managing other high-priority responsibilities. How can you find enough time to do it all and communicate effectively?

Have colleagues or team members review your communications before sending them. Be sure to articulate your message, questions, or status up front, in as few words as possible. Take time to consider your communication from the perspective of the recipient. Leave nothing vague.

KEY TAKEAWAYS

✓ Confirm and document receipt of your communications.

✓ Craft every word you use and think how it might be interpreted.

✓ Make your point using the fewest words possible.

✓ Have colleagues review important communications.

ROMEO'S FATE AND THE PROBLEM OF UNANSWERED EMAILS

The tragedy of Shakespeare's *Romeo and Juliet* hinges on the smallest of things: a missed message. As anyone familiar with the story knows, Juliet is separated from Romeo and agrees to an elaborate plan where she takes a potion that puts her in a coma so that people will think she is dead. When she wakes, she will run away with Romeo, where their families can never bother them again. It's a daring scheme, and a messenger is sent to tell Romeo what is going on—but he doesn't reach him in time.

Instead, poor Romeo hears that Juliet is dead and drinks poison to join her. That terrible outcome could have been avoided if she hadn't assumed that Romeo would get the message. When in doubt, make sure to get a direct confirmation from the recipient. If you don't, you can't be sure your message has been seen or heard.

In the modern business world, messages get missed all the time, and projects suffer for it. Simply sending an email isn't enough, especially when an important task is on the line. How can you be sure it was read? How do you know it didn't go into the spam folder? Too often team members use passive forms of communication such as email and voicemail and don't get a response. It's not the recipient's fault—the burden of communication is squarely on the sender's shoulders. If you don't get a response, do what it takes to confirm that the message was received.

If one form of messaging isn't drawing a response from your recipient, use other methods to confirm and verify that your message was received, seen, and understood. If that person works with you in the same building, it might be necessary to ditch various digital efforts altogether and just have a face-to-face exchange with them. Always take a proactive approach.

KEY TAKEAWAYS

✓ Be proactive and find effective methods to communicate with colleagues and stakeholders.

✓ Exhaust all possible methods, from phone calls to face-to-face meetings, to confirm that your message is received and understood.

✓ Be transparent in your communication by copying the team on emails and underscoring the importance of their response.

✓ Get a response before relieving yourself of your responsibility to communicate.

KNOW WHEN TO SPEAK UP

Novelist and short-story writer Sherwood Anderson, in a letter to a friend, remembered old farmers in his hometown of Camden, Ohio, "speaking feelingly of an evening spent on the big, empty plains of the Midwest. It had taken the shrillness out of them. They had learned the trick of quiet."[36]

People often speak up because they are uncomfortable with silence or with a long gap in a discussion, or because they feel the need to be heard, even when they don't have anything valuable to add. As a result, they restate or agree with what has already been said, and time is wasted.

Measured silence can speak volumes. People who are usually silent are the ones truly heard when they do elect to speak. Be selective in what you say and when you speak. Knowing when to speak is an acquired trait, but one well worth cultivating.

Knowing when to speak lends value to what you say and allows you to make meaningful contributions to a conversation. By holding back until you are ready to speak, you will stand out and command the attention of your audience.

KEY TAKEAWAYS

✓ Knowing when to speak up and when to stay quiet is an acquired skill.

✓ Be selective about when you speak so what you say has gravitas.

✓ You don't have to agree with, or repeat, what people say to be heard.

CASE STUDY

SUMMARY

Setting expectations requires clear communications. Most challenges and problems occur because expectations aren't conveyed, which leaves team members to formulate their own opinions of what is expected. Often the results are mixed, leaving your stakeholders unhappy. Clearly communicating expectations is critical to defining what success looks like. That means outlining the responsibilities of each team member so that everyone understands what they need to do to contribute to the overall success of the project. And to be effective, it requires communicating facts, regardless of particular sensitivities or prevailing politics.

PROBLEM

A healthcare client experienced a large influx of more than sixty medium- to large-scale clinical information systems projects. At the same time, they were dealing with resourcing issues, a breakdown in communications, and a lack of overall coordination. The result was that the client was not meeting its goals and time lines to deliver on these initiatives.

SOLUTION

T2 helped the client's clinical information systems team develop a structure to regularly review project status, work through roadblocks, prioritize, and review new project intake. This structure established a necessary cadence for daily, weekly, and monthly communication. It featured regular portfolio-review meetings that included stakeholders, project managers, training staff, organizational-change management, and clinical analysts to create better communication and transparency across teams. Meetings pushed not only project managers but also analysts and other team members to take ownership of their projects and speak up to make sure everyone was aware of issues, risks, and concerns. By coordinating closely, the teams were able to make decisions more efficiently, avoid over-allocation of key resources to different areas, and ensure that all team members were aware of all the projects currently in progress. Furthermore, T2 helped establish an overall executive governance structure that allowed the clinical information systems leadership to funnel necessary items to key stakeholders and assist with prioritization across the board.

TEAMWORK

It might seem self-evident, but it bears repeating: no shared project can succeed without effective teamwork. And in order to foster that as a project manager, you must **know your team.** By discerning what each team member can contribute and embracing their different attitudes and perspectives, you will have at your disposal a fount of critical thinking that is invaluable for the project's success.

When gathering your team together, instill among the members a sense of shared accountability that fosters **unity,** promotes engaged collaboration, and encourages increased commitment. **Capitalize on the team's expertise** by tapping into the rich knowledge that they possess. **Nurture open, civil discussion** to reap the full reward.

Advise team members that shared accountability means trusting others on the team to take **responsibility.** Coach them to step out of their comfort zones and **feel the pain** of growth through trial and error as they combine their strengths to arrive at the right solution. If a single team member doesn't perform well, ask that other members of the team offer assistance rather than **place blame.** This often applies to **new team**

members, who can't be expected to adjust instantly to a new management style and must be integrated incrementally.

Every problem between team members is a **team problem.** When there is a conflict between two members, it affects all team members, so to create a positive resolution, other members must get involved. Quite often, they will bring less emotion to the subject and fresh perspectives that the individuals in the dispute just don't see. Beware of any member with **selfish tendencies** who may be opposed to creating a team environment that supports professionalism for all. Take action to protect the team by managing any sense of entitlement.

Although by its very definition, teamwork assumes a plurality, and differences in various team members' way of thinking contribute to the strength of the whole, the team must take care to speak with **one voice** to stakeholders. Even if the project is a success, the impression of disagreement among team members could hurt a stakeholder's confidence.

Such a unified voice is developed through regular **collaboration** of team members away from the eyes of stakeholders. With robust, respectful debate, the team can innovate, compromise, and reach a **consensus** to solve problems and achieve goals. In this way, every team member can own the commitment and take responsibility for it as a team.

KNOW YOUR TEAM MEMBERS

In 1860, Abraham Lincoln was determined to recruit the ablest men for his cabinet, including former rivals who ran against him for the presidency. "I had looked the party over and concluded that these were the very strongest men," Lincoln said.[37] By putting his cabinet together in this way, Lincoln gained access to a wider range of opinions than if he had chosen loyalists.

Everyone has a different yet valid perspective—and strength—to offer. And it's up to you to know what each of your team members can offer during the course of a project. This requires that you consider all perspectives as different opinions arise within the group and decisions evolve. Encourage everyone to contribute and consider one another's viewpoints, especially attitudes or conclusions that differ from their own. Remember that while your team may be in unanimous agreement about what the end result of a project will look like, there could be many different approaches to help you get there.

When you know what each team member can contribute and you all embrace differing attitudes and perspectives, the sheer variety of thought that results can be invaluable to the success of a project.

KEY TAKEAWAYS

✓ Consider all perspectives as your opinions and decisions evolve.
✓ Encourage team members to see and understand one another's perspectives.
✓ Embrace attitudes that differ from your own.
✓ Understand why differences exist between team members.

BUILD UNITY

Early Greek history chronicles how Lycurgus founded the first Spartan army and created a force where no soldier was considered superior to another. He developed mastery in the Spartans through the army's foundation of endurance, courage, and self-control. Fighting in a phalanx formation was an ancient Greek style of battle that was adopted by the Spartans. Just like in an ideal project team, the phalanx worked as a unit in a close, deep formation and made coordinated mass maneuvers.

With a variety of components needed to move a project forward, it's common to divide tasks among individual team members and hold them accountable for their portion of the project. But does this work?

Shift your operational mode and team dynamic to one holding the entire team accountable for results. This instills a sense of unity in the team, promotes engaged collaboration, and increases commitment among members.

KEY TAKEAWAYS

- ✓ Encourage team collaboration by having team members partner together.
- ✓ Urge team members to seek and offer help to one another throughout each project iteration.
- ✓ Allow team members to provide input that is free of judgment.
- ✓ Hold your entire team accountable for results.

CAPITALIZE ON THE TEAM'S EXPERTISE

In most sports, coaches give their team guidance and strategy leading up to each game and make adjustments during timeouts. Then the team members deliver their autonomous and specialized expertise as they work together to win—usually against a ticking clock.

As a project manager, emulate the coach model, and tap into the knowledge-rich resource that is your team. Outline the project requirements for them. Let them be in charge of their commitments. They should know what it takes, and the timeline required to achieve goals. Empower them to succeed or fail without overdirecting them. Let them give you guidance on what needs to be done. When you value their input, team members feel more involved, respected, and invested in winning the game.

Build a culture in which the members of your team are invested in one another and respected by the organization. Your team members have the skills and knowledge needed to execute their objectives and estimate how long it will take them. Empower your team by capitalizing on its existing expertise and allow the team to self-manage.

KEY TAKEAWAYS

- ✓ Allow the team to work together to determine what is required to get a project done.
- ✓ Have the team estimate how long tasks will take to complete.
- ✓ Empower the team to be accountable, and they will be more invested in the project's success.
- ✓ Allow the team to manage themselves and become self-sufficient.

TEAMWORK

NURTURE OPEN, CIVIL DISCUSSION

When Greek and Roman messengers went to deliver information to other countries, it was a tradition to bring along an olive branch. Especially when the messenger was delivering bad news, the branch was a reminder that the messenger was there on behalf of someone else. The branch signaled that the messenger was not to blame for his words and shouldn't be punished.

This ancient tradition ensured that envoys would speak candidly, regardless of who was listening to them. Times may have changed, but the necessity for candor and honesty remains. Project success depends on the creation of a sense of safety and nonjudgment during any team discussion.

Too often team members withhold their honest views about a project's goals, especially if the client or another important stakeholder is in the room. This dynamic contradicts one of the most important tenets of the Agile philosophy: the need to speak plainly and openly for the good of the team.

It's human nature to play to one's audience, especially when that audience includes important, influential members. But to mitigate the influence—however unintended—of having an important member in the room, plan a separate meeting with the team to discuss issues and come to a consensus.

KEY TAKEAWAYS

- ✓ Be honest and transparent in all your communication regardless of what you are communicating.
- ✓ Always refer to any message as coming from the team as a whole.
- ✓ Reach consensus with the team before meeting with top stakeholders.

ENTRUST OTHERS WITH RESPONSIBILITY

In *The Hardest Job in the World: The American Presidency,* journalist John Dickerson relates that President Dwight D. Eisenhower didn't like to be given unopened letters. Even though his staff thought that they were respecting his privacy, Eisenhower didn't appreciate the gesture.[38]

Why? The former Allied commander of the D-Day invasion was a very practical person, and highly time-conscious. He insisted on having all of his letters vetted by his staff so that he wouldn't receive anything that would turn out to be unimportant and waste his time. Nothing better shows the importance of trust in a team than Eisenhower's attitude. By trusting his staff to determine what deserved his attention, the commander-in-chief freed himself to deal with more important members and empowered his subordinates. When this kind of trust takes place on a team, it opens the way to more efficiency and success. When team members respect one another enough to allow others to make important decisions on their behalf, the team rises to a higher level.

Encourage your team to trust one another and to understand everyone's roles. Being truly efficient means allowing other team members to take responsibility from you. The more that you can instill a trusting attitude in your team, the better you can develop a culture of successful collaboration and efficiency.

KEY TAKEAWAYS

✓ Learn to optimize everybody's role on your team.

✓ Entrust your team members with the power to make decisions.

✓ When team members learn to trust one another, they free others to fulfill their full potential.

LET YOUR TEAM FEEL THE PAIN

In the gym, it's the "burn" that brings more powerful muscles. While exercisers may initially resist the discomfort, once they push through the pain and see how success feels, they're back for more.

The best project managers are mentors and growth coaches. One of their greatest challenges is guiding team members to become masters of their own destiny by teaching them new ways of thinking and working. Encouraging team members to step out of their comfort zones, take ownership, and support accomplishment as a team will inspire a growth mindset. Be patient as they adjust to succeeding by working through the pain and adapting to productive change.

Your team members all come with proven individual strengths and skills, but now, you need them to work as a single unit that communicates as one. How do you bring them together as a unified team?

Coach and mentor your team to experience success together by arriving at the right solution through the pain of trial and error. The process will empower the team, teach them to be accountable, and allow them to become self-sufficient, which promotes growth for the individuals as well as the organization.

KEY TAKEAWAYS

✓ Begin by using small iterations so your team can experience success early.

✓ Allow your team to succeed or fail on their own.

✓ Make sure stakeholders know that the entire team working in tandem is responsible for success, rather than individual members.

EVERYONE SUFFERS WHEN
TEAM MEMBERS PLACE BLAME

In 2015, the Washington Nationals arguably had one of Major League Baseball's most talented rosters, but they failed to make the playoffs. At the bottom of the eighth inning in a tied game against the Philadelphia Phillies, pitcher Jonathan Papelbon expressed frustration with Bryce Harper for his poor performance at bat, which led to a physical altercation in the dugout between the two teammates. The game ended with a victory for the Phillies, who beat the Nationals 12–5. To add to the team's woes, Papelbon was suspended for four games, ending his season.

Your team's interpersonal conflicts may not rise to the level of the Harper–Papelbon feud, but any time team members prefer fighting and fault-finding over helping one another, project success and team productivity are bound to suffer. When a single member doesn't perform well—and it happens often—it's up to the rest of the team to adjust and help them, not find fault. Convey to the team that they can be more productive and effective working with one another than they can working against one another.

The success of the project rests on everyone's shoulders, not on any individual, so make sure that team cohesiveness is one of your top priorities.

Fault-finding creates a negative atmosphere that always hurts team success. Instead, have everyone make a conscious decision to help one another out. Team cohesiveness is vital.

KEY TAKEAWAYS

✓ Encourage team members to help one another rather than criticize.

✓ Remind your team that the goal is accountability as a team.

✓ Create a culture of mutual respect and collegiality.

✓ Focus on sending the message that the individuals in your group will always be stronger when working as a team.

AVOID A CULTURE CLASH WHEN A NEW MEMBER JOINS YOUR TEAM

Some of the most common problems that a new college student faces have nothing to do with the classroom. Rather, they arise from the novel characteristics of college life: freedom, new responsibilities, greater self-accountability, and the loneliness of being an outsider in a strange new world.

A similar dynamic is often at work when a new employee arrives. They may have trouble adjusting if they've left a top-down organization that doesn't practice team decision-making or reaching consensus. The two management cultures couldn't be more different. How will the new team member handle it? No matter how willing they are to change, the new person can't do it alone: it's up to the team to help them.

One of the hardest adjustments is getting comfortable with disclosing problems at team meetings and at the end of iterations. In traditional situations, most people are taught to hide weaknesses to avoid criticism. But new employees must be helped—and it will take time and patience—to realize that honesty and transparency are necessary for high-performing teams. That includes changing their vocabulary. Help new team members shift from focusing on individual accomplishments toward describing what the team accomplishes instead.

No one should be expected to adjust overnight to a new management style and culture. This is one of the greatest challenges facing any team, and it's a major reason why many fail. Helping a new team member to change their mindset and behavior is a gradual process.

KEY TAKEAWAYS

✓ Make sure that the team doesn't judge the new team member.

✓ Emphasize transparency to encourage the new person to share problems.

✓ Help new members shift away from self-centered language to a team-centered vocabulary and mindset.

✓ Help new members understand that they're not on their own and should rely on their colleagues for help.

EVERY PROBLEM IS A TEAM PROBLEM

When it comes to conflicts between two people, teams play an invaluable role. The zone defense in basketball illustrates why. It's different from man-to-man defense in that, instead of guarding a particular player, each defender guards a "zone" or section of the court and any opponent that comes into that area. The entire team shifts its position in relation to the ball. No defender is ever left on their own: the team moves and protects the basket together.

In business environments, especially when there are conflicts between two members, it's useful to employ a zone defense. In typical situations, people tend to avoid other people's conflicts. *It's not my problem*, they think. Wrong! When a project depends on team cohesiveness and consensus, it's everyone's problem.

To create a positive resolution, your team must get involved and share in the disagreement. Having everyone take part in the issue and its resolution puts a focus on team dynamics over individual ones, just like the zone defense. Often teams will bring fresh perspectives—and less emotion—to a conflict that the individuals involved wouldn't see otherwise.

Problems among a team's members are always team problems and must be aired collectively. It's important to shift the focus of member conflicts from an individual mindset to a team mindset. At the end of the day, it's always the team that drives success—the team is accountable, not either individual.

KEY TAKEAWAYS

✓ Focus on team accountability. Working as a team means addressing problems as a team.

✓ Hold meetings for every iteration to boost consensus and catch problems early.

✓ To reach consensus, discuss member conflicts as a team.

✓ To change member mindsets, allow your team to share in the disagreement.

BAN SELFISHNESS ON THE TEAM

What happens when there's a narcissist on your team? Nothing good, warns Manfred Kets de Vries in the *Harvard Business Review*. Many teams—too many, he says—struggle with individuals who think their past experiences and successful track records give them a special position of importance above everyone else.[39]

That sense of entitlement might be hidden (at least initially) behind friendly, charismatic behavior, but eventually these individuals create too much stress and tension for the team. Managers might try to stop them, but often this intervention takes place after the damage has been done.

What is this damage? It isn't necessarily a failed project or poor results. In fact, the job might be successfully completed, because that troublesome individual has excellent skills. The real harm lies elsewhere: when one person dominates a project, the rest of the team doesn't have a chance to grow or learn.

To avoid this, set a tone of consensus and transparency at the project's beginning. Be vocal and repetitive with this message, giving a clear signal to any potentially problematic members that their behavior won't be tolerated. Such messaging also underscores the value of every team member's voice regardless of their experience level.

Remember that there is an ethical dimension to building a team that learns and grows. Be wary of any member who seems opposed to creating a team environment that supports professional self-improvement. Don't let these individuals limit the team's chance for success.

KEY TAKEAWAYS

✓ Emphasize the value of every team member's point of view, regardless of their experience level.

✓ Illustrate the benefits of enabling the team to learn and grow.

✓ Manage a team member's sense of entitlement if necessary.

✓ Encourage the team to be accountable in resolving a problem with a team member or requesting their removal.

SPEAK WITH ONE VOICE

One of the most interesting forms of behavior in the insect world has come to be known, in the words of animal behaviorist Thomas Seeley, as "honeybee democracy." A swarm of bees functions so effectively as a group that the average observer doesn't realize that the swarm is a democracy, where disagreement and vigorous debate occur among the bees every year as they search for a new home for their hive and queen.

Even though team members don't always agree with one another, it's important to present a picture of team unity—just like one sees in bee colonies—to various project stakeholders. No matter how much debate or disagreement happens in your team, it's important to strike a balance. The group must speak with one voice to the outside world.

The problem is that sometimes teams forget this rule. When that happens, a variety of stakeholders will learn about conflicts that should have been left in the conference room. Don't air your team's dirty laundry. Even if the project is a terrific success, the impression of team disagreement could still undermine your stakeholders' confidence.

Debate is a necessary part of every team's function, but keep knowledge of it within the team. A fundamental principle of the Agile philosophy is agreement. Don't finalize a major decision point that doesn't reflect team consensus.

KEY TAKEAWAYS

- ✓ Don't publicly contradict fellow team members.
- ✓ Be accountable and responsible, as a team, for all decisions and results.
- ✓ Encourage team transparency, but use discretion with outside stakeholders.
- ✓ Achieve consensus about how team results should be communicated to stakeholders.

COLLABORATE REGULARLY

Director Akira Kurosawa's legendary movie *Rashomon* is famous for a plot device that involves various characters—eyewitnesses to a harrowing event—remembering the same incident in different ways. The idea of people interpreting an event from completely different perspectives is often called "the Rashomon effect."[40]

That effect can be put to good use by having a team collaborate on a problem. People seldom think about a problem the exact same way, so by actively asking for input and opinions from team members who might think slightly differently, many perspectives and approaches can be explored, almost always leading to a workable solution. Increased collaboration means enhanced value.

If you want to become innovative in your thinking, encourage individuals to have divergent ideas. The feedback you'll get through this method of collaboration will lead to consensus and a strong, unified approach to problem solving that everyone agrees on.

KEY TAKEAWAYS

✓ Work as a team to gain different perspectives on the same problem.

✓ Don't think that you, as a single individual, have all the answers.

✓ Different perspectives can lead to a coherent, unified approach to a problem.

REACH A TEAM CONSENSUS

On September 11, 2001, Todd Beamer, a passenger on United Airlines Flight 93, spoke on the phone with a customer service representative to alert them that his flight had been hijacked and that he and some of the other passengers had discussed what to do. After learning what had just happened at the World Trade Center and the Pentagon, Beamer and others on board reached a consensus. They would try to prevent the hijackers from crashing the plane into their intended target, thought to have been the White House. Beamer's last audible words—"Let's roll!"—became a national catchphrase.[41]

True success in any project can only happen when a team comes together as a unified whole and acts as one. For that to occur, team members must reach a consensus even if compromises are made. Debate should be allowed free rein, and opinions and decisions respected.

It's possible, even probable, that people will disagree with one another during the free flow of ideas. That's OK. It's important, however, that after such give-and-take, everyone agrees to support the consensus that's been reached.

Strive for inclusiveness when forming a consensus, even when opinions differ. Stand firm as a team and support the consensus after it is reached via discussion and debate.

KEY TAKEAWAYS

✓ Reach a consensus as to what needs to be done and by what date.

✓ Ask team members to collaborate and debate freely among themselves.

✓ If compromise is necessary, be united in your final decision as a team.

✓ Act as if every decision or opinion is yours.

CASE STUDY

SUMMARY

Superior teamwork leverages all the team's skills and the full value that each member has to offer. When that convergence is achieved, the team unites as a single entity, all accountable to one another, failing or succeeding together. And, as a single entity, the team is then accountable to stakeholders or project owners.

PROBLEM

A client needed to bring its application and infrastructure departments together to help complete a multiyear migration of four hundred applications to a new data center. Culturally, for many organizations, applications and infrastructure teams have a myopic perspective, and they normally work as separate teams that come together only when they have to. This normal mode of "collaboration" for a project of this scale and visibility would have been problematic and produced poor outcomes. The success of this project required both departments—each having more than two hundred employees—to work together as a single team and be accountable to the organization as a whole.

SOLUTION

T2 assisted the client in dividing the four hundred applications across twelve teams of approximately ten employees each. The teams were spread out over multiple departments, creating cross-functional teams composed of applications owners, infrastructure architects, project managers, and security specialists. The teams were then tasked with migrating their respective twenty-plus applications. The teams reported as a single entity, thereby making them accountable to one another. This collaboration was the driving force that made the project successful.

STANDARDS

The value of standards in project management is inestimable. Without such benchmarks for success, achieving goals, satisfying stakeholders, and maintaining focus and cohesion among team members would be impossible.

The importance of a uniform set of standards comes into particularly fine focus when **establishing procedures and rules.** Life runs on rules and procedures, but they are useless unless everyone operating under them understands what they cover and agrees to abide by them. A business run without rules and procedures—just improvised off the cuff—would be self-defeating and utterly chaotic. Perhaps the most critical cog in any business, processes are designed to help an enterprise function with optimal results. When followed consistently, an **effective process** provides a measure of productivity and performance, helping a company evolve.

While setting high standards is admirable, don't set yourself up to fail when committing to goals. **Be realistic** about what you and your team can achieve. Setting impossible goals not only disappoints stakeholders—it demoralizes the team. When there is a divide between a stakeholder request and what your team can deliver, as the team's advocate, it's your job to find the **middle ground.** It's vital at all times that you **be clear about**

what is expected, even if it makes for an uncomfortable conversation. In rare, worst-case scenarios, when mediation and all mitigating efforts have failed, it may be necessary to terminate a project. Regardless of who may be right or wrong, **never burn bridges.** Always treat colleagues and stakeholders with respect and professionalism.

On the other hand, if requirements change and a project must be redefined, don't be risk-averse. Just make sure you **know how to adapt** and mitigate exposures aligning with your scope, cost, and timeline. See change as an opportunity for growth and document the lessons learned—lessons that may be incorporated as standards later.

No matter how tight deadlines get, remember that **slowing down** to reassess and make adjustments actually helps to maintain, or even increase, momentum and to produce a high-quality result. In addition, all work and no play makes Jack a dull boy, so enhance productivity by injecting an element of **fun** into team meetings. Games can tap into team members' creative and imaginative faculties in unexpected ways and produce solutions to challenges that have never been considered before.

While there is always room for improvement to any task, there comes a point when further refinement jeopardizes necessary momentum. The solution? Get very precise about the project and **clarify when done means done!** Just keep in mind that the one standard that should never be undermined is the quality of the end result. **Being the best you can** shouldn't be negotiable.

ESTABLISH PROCEDURES AND RULES

On the night of April 14, 1912, the RMS *Titanic*, on its maiden voyage, hit an iceberg and sank. In total, 1,503 people died, many needlessly. In part, these deaths occurred because rules and procedures were disregarded. Contrary to procedure, the *Titanic* ignored several iceberg warnings before it slammed into one. Because the rules governing them were out-of-date, the ship had too few lifeboats. And of the lifeboats that were launched, many were under capacity, rescuing only 705 people when nearly 500 more could have been saved had better procedures been in place.

Critical operations or important initiatives are governed by rules and processes, but they are useless unless you agree on what they cover and abide by them. One of the responsibilities of a project manager is to see that rules and procedures are followed.

Making rules and processes work takes practice. It's also important for coworkers to remind one another of what those rules and procedures actually mean. Being consistent and predictable in establishing and following guidelines makes it easier to stay in alignment with them. Sometimes rules and processes require change. When they do, make sure to reach a team agreement about if and how they should be altered and change them together.

Rules and processes are essential to any team or business. They exist to be followed, but if they need to be amended, do not do it arbitrarily. Form a consensus and then make the changes.

KEY TAKEAWAYS

✓ Practice following the rules you and your team set.

✓ Remind team members of the rules and why they are important.

✓ Be consistent and predictable with how you apply the standards and rules.

✓ If needed, change rules together, and have a clear understanding of why you are making the changes.

THE IMPORTANCE OF
EFFECTIVE PROCESSES

Henry Ford didn't invent the automobile or the assembly line. But more than any other person, he was responsible for transforming the automobile from a costly product that catered to the rich into a machine that shaped the twentieth century. By 1910, his production process took a mere ninety-three minutes, and Ford was producing more cars than all other automakers combined with only a fraction of the workers.[42]

Working without effective processes is like trying to keep your balance on a bed of quicksand. It's impossible because the ground is constantly shifting under your feet. Good processes are at the root of any successful enterprise or team. They exist to help your business and team function correctly, evolve, and optimize results. With a stable foundation of processes, you can also accurately measure productivity and performance. By establishing that foundation early, you will foster good discipline, allow for repetition when needed, and guard against misinterpretation.

A process with firm footing—that can also be tweaked for better results when needed—establishes a foundation from which a team can evolve. It is perhaps one of the most critical components of any team or business.

KEY TAKEAWAYS

✓ Establish a foundation that can evolve and be optimized over time.

✓ Enforce discipline and look for opportunities to improve the process for the better.

✓ Define your purpose so misinterpretation doesn't occur.

✓ Measure your productivity and performance.

BALANCE PROJECT GOALS WITH A HEALTHY DOSE OF REALISM

In the annals of man-made disasters, China's Great Leap Forward is one of the greatest. Chairman Mao's push for a rapid transformation and modernization of his country devastated it instead, with at least 30 million people dying of starvation.

It isn't always a big goal that causes problems. Rather, it's an unwillingness to drill down into the details that often leads to disaster. In Mao's case, his attempt to turn peasants into small-scale industrialists overnight was doomed by its own overzealousness. China's fragile agricultural system simply could not bear Mao's massive, poorly considered changes and collapsed. It's a grim warning to any project management team that failure is guaranteed whenever you ignore details and don't establish a reasonable cadence for tasks.

Communication is vital. When an entire team comes together and focuses on project details, a fuller, more accurate picture of what's achievable becomes clear. With consensus and cooperation guiding the team, lofty goals can be scaled into sensible, successful iterations.

Setting impossible goals not only disappoints stakeholders, it demoralizes the team. That doesn't mean that the bar must be set low on all tasks: just be realistic about what's possible. If your team happens to exceed expectations, that's terrific! But don't set them up for failure before the task even starts.

KEY TAKEAWAYS

✓ Be practical about time, team capabilities, and stakeholder expectations.

✓ Teach success to your team by defining realistic goals.

✓ Lofty goals can be achieved when scaled down into sensible iterations.

FIND THE MIDDLE GROUND

Camp David, just sixty-four miles from Washington, DC, has been used by American presidents as a negotiating site since FDR invited Winston Churchill there in 1943. A long procession of dignitaries—from the USSR's Nikita Khrushchev, to the Palestinian Liberation Organization's Yasser Arafat—have gone there to work out political conflicts in a rustic setting with help from various American presidents.

The power of mediation doesn't belong only to heads of state. Every team and project potentially need mediation help, especially when a team reaches a consensus that the stakeholder might not like. What happens if they disagree with your team's result? The project manager needs to step in and mediate.

Although it's natural to want to be in agreement with your stakeholders, your team may need to do the opposite to successfully meet the project objectives. In addition to clearly communicating with the team about stakeholder expectations, the project manager or task leader should be an advocate for the team when discussing their results with the project sponsors.

A project manager or task leader has a responsibility to inform but not necessarily to please. As uncomfortable as this might seem, this role is a necessary part of the project process. It establishes an important channel of honest feedback between the team and sponsors.

KEY TAKEAWAYS

- ✓ Understand stakeholders' needs, wants, and preferences.
- ✓ Develop consensus about project plans and designs within your team.
- ✓ Resolve differences internally, requesting input from stakeholders as needed.
- ✓ Establish as-needed meetings between stakeholders and the team to inform and clearly present each party's point of view to mediate disagreements.

DON'T ASSUME:
BE CLEAR ABOUT EXPECTATIONS

NASA lost a Mars Climate Orbiter on September 23, 1999, as it went into orbital insertion over the Red Planet. An investigation attributed the failure to a piece of software in charge of the orbiter's thrusters that failed to convert from imperial to metric units. This mistake led to the loss of a 125 million dollar mission.[43]

The pitfalls of not spelling out expectations clearly—a fault that many teams experience during the project process—can lead to circumstances as dire as what NASA faced. Miscommunications, assumptions, and a lack of specificity among team members about deadlines and related expectations can quickly translate into failure.

No one intends to fail on purpose. Most of the time, it happens because team members didn't understand what was expected of them in the first place. It's critical to be explicit about expectations for a particular task from the outset. Don't assume that everyone will understand your requirements for a task and its urgency if you don't state it. Team members need to be similarly explicit when these expectations are too vague. They need to resist the temptation to promise particular results when they don't understand what is actually being asked of them.

Clear and explicit communications about requirements are vital to successful task completion. Be honest about them, even if it makes for an uncomfortable conversation. It's far better to be uncomfortable than to build something that will fail to meet its objective.

KEY TAKEAWAYS

✓ State requirements with clear, explicit language.

✓ Ask detailed questions about the task. Who's doing what? When can it be completed?

✓ Don't pretend to understand to please someone. When you fail, it will be a greater embarrassment, and will weaken their trust in you.

END A PROJECT, BUT DON'T BURN BRIDGES

A common tactic of ancient Roman military commanders was to destroy bridges. Sometimes this was done to stop the enemy from fleeing. In other situations, the commanders actually used this tactic on their own legions. Bridges were destroyed—and sometimes boats, too—behind their armies so there was no way to retreat. The message was clear: win the battle and press on—or die trying.

This problematic behavior—in projects, business, and life in general—of "burning one's bridges" is something that can't be undone and makes returning to a past relationship nearly impossible. Constructive communication, mutual respect, and transparency are crucial to avoiding this situation with a project stakeholder or a team member.

Establishing transparency between your team and your stakeholder on day one is especially helpful in less-than-ideal situations when it might be necessary to call it quits. If the stakeholder has known all along that the team has had trouble with the goal, they won't be surprised when the team decides that it isn't the right fit and needs to walk away from the iteration.

When it's time to make a break, avoid personal feelings or opinions. They don't add value because they don't provide any helpful information. Instead, stick to the facts and choose your words carefully. Remember that tone is critical.

KEY TAKEAWAYS

- ✓ When transparency and mutual respect are present from the beginning, burning bridges will never be an issue.
- ✓ Regardless of who is right or wrong, never burn bridges. Rather, treat all colleagues and stakeholders with respect and professionalism.
- ✓ Remember that the world is small. End all engagements with thanks for what was done.
- ✓ If you're providing feedback to the stakeholder, focus on the facts. Your opinion, unless it's valuable, is not necessary.

ADAPT FOR PROJECT SUCCESS

David Wallerstein was annoyed. He'd tried everything. A young executive at a movie chain in the 1960s, he wanted to boost concession profits. The theater concessions stand is the real source of revenue for most theaters, and Wallerstein had tried two-for-one deals and matinee specials. Nothing worked and profits stayed the same. Then he had an epiphany: people were just too embarrassed to be seen eating two bags of popcorn. To solve the problem, he simply created a larger bag, and the jumbo size was born.[44]

When requirements change and a project needs to be redefined, a mature project team will find ways to adapt to the challenge, just as Wallerstein did. You can't stick to an old schedule or budget if the situation has evolved. That's a common mistake made by many teams—a reluctance to let go of the original strategy even if it doesn't fit the situation anymore.

In a dynamic environment, sticking to an outdated understanding of a problem will cause you to miss out on new opportunities. Rather than grow frustrated with a changing situation, encourage your team to treat the changes as an opportunity for learning and growth.

Frequently check in with the project sponsor to ensure that your team's goals are still aligned with stakeholder expectations. Avoid performing detailed planning too early in areas where the scope is likely to change. That way there will be less resistance to change from the team when it inevitably happens.

KEY TAKEAWAYS

- ✓ Proceed with short iterations so that you get early feedback on necessary changes.
- ✓ Identify the effect on the project of changes taking place in the business.
- ✓ Don't be risk-averse, just make sure you know how to adapt and mitigate exposures.
- ✓ See change as an opportunity for growth, and document lessons learned.

SLOW DOWN TO GO FASTER

A lawsuit filed against Boeing over the flawed 737 Max alleges that in its rush to get the jet plane to market, Boeing did not properly test the new system or adequately train pilots.[45] Boeing denies this, but with the amount of time it has taken to correct the problem, one could argue that had they *gone slower to go faster*, they might not have had the problems they encountered.

Reports have come out claiming that Boeing's rush to compete with the Airbus A320 ended up costing around 20 billion dollars and grounded 790 planes. As any effective team should know, when the pressure's on, it never pays to cut corners. Sometimes it may even be necessary to say "no" and walk away—or, in Boeing's case, to scale back their goals.

It may seem counterintuitive, but slowing down actually helps with maintaining momentum and producing a high-quality product or result. Why? It gives your team a chance to reassess and make adjustments so that everyone is clear about their goals. Such care and attention spare the team from having to rework problems later, and that translates into major time savings.

Quality is never negotiable. If stakeholder expectations threaten this, it may be necessary to say "no." It is better to be up front and clarify that a stakeholder's request to cut corners is going to actually slow the project down because of rework rather than to allow the corner-cutting and then fail to deliver a usable outcome.

KEY TAKEAWAYS

- ✓ Conduct regular status updates with your team, even when deadlines are looming.
- ✓ Resist the impulse to just rush ahead. Wait until verification is completed.
- ✓ Maintain high standards of quality to avoid extensive reworking later.
- ✓ Don't be afraid to tell stakeholders no if their request for acceleration will undermine quality and lead to rework.

ENHANCE PRODUCTIVITY BY MAKING MEETINGS FUN

When some people hear the phrase "Dungeons and Dragons," they imagine a group of shy teenagers rolling odd-looking dice in a dimly lit basement. But the popular 1974 role-playing game and its many imitators have been recognized by the project management world as something else: an example of the power of team building.[46]

Draw on the inspiration of such games for your team's next retrospective meeting or planning session. When you do, it can have a big, positive effect on what happens. Sometimes team members are reluctant to share, and the energy in the room isn't what it needs to be. Games change that energy. Introducing an element of fun can improve the outcome of the whole meeting.

Use games to build team member interactions and get creative juices flowing. Introducing some competition never hurts. But take note: the competition should be friendly—the goal isn't to pit team members against one another. If that happens, everything could backfire; you're liable to ruin the interpersonal bonds that are supposed to be developed in these sessions.

Management experts agree that the use of gamification, especially in business settings, can tap into team members' creative and imaginative faculties in unexpected ways and produce novel solutions. Used in the right way, an element of play assists in team building and productivity.

KEY TAKEAWAYS

- ✓ Create a meeting environment that fosters bonding among team members.
- ✓ Introduce fun into meetings through the use of game-style approaches to solving challenges. Your team will be more open as a result.
- ✓ Encourage friendly competition during meetings to get the feedback flowing.

WHAT DOES *DONE* REALLY MEAN?

Leonardo da Vinci said that "Art is never finished, only abandoned." This might be interpreted as a command to constantly look to improve your work and always aim for perfection. It may also be simply acknowledging a reality: you can always go back and try to improve what you have done. This could be one of the reasons Leonardo had so much unfinished work.

Sure, there's always room for improvement to any task, but there comes a point when further refinement seriously hurts momentum. The solution? Get very specific about the project. When goals and objectives aren't clearly defined, teams don't know when a task is actually complete. Providing focused answers to three critical questions—*What am I doing? Why am I doing it? Who is it for?*—will enable them to move to the next step and not look back again. No more tweaking or fine-tuning. Done means done.

Teams often struggle with uncertainty about whether or not a task is sufficiently completed. They need clear information to help them measure progress and reach a satisfactory level of completion. Spare them unnecessary tension and confusion by making sure that the criteria for each task are clearly stated at the beginning.

KEY TAKEAWAYS

✓ Make sure to answer the three Ws—What?, Why?, and Who?—before you begin any task.

✓ Narrow your descriptions of tasks to make them as clear as possible.

✓ Refine your scope so you can get the task done in a short iteration.

✓ Remember, done means done. If the task was well defined, then you should never have to go back to the same task.

BE THE BEST YOU CAN BE

Dr. Martin Luther King Jr. gave an old poem new life when he incorporated it into a speech in 1967. "Be a bush if you can't be a tree. If you can't be a highway, just be a trail. If you can't be a sun, be a star. For it isn't by size that you win or fail. Be the best of whatever you are."[47] Dr. King knew fifty years ago that the poem's message was ageless and universal.

People have a tendency to cut corners in whatever they do. It's natural. They look for the easiest way out. You can always find a way to get things done on time and on budget by altering plans and perhaps scaling back the project. But delivering a high-quality product is an absolute and should never be compromised.

You can't undercut quality if you want to be the best at what you do. You should always go the extra mile in delivering a superior product no matter what constraints are affecting the work process. Putting a premium on quality sets you apart, as does working slower to be faster and doing things just once.

The idea of being the best you can be is nonnegotiable. In fact, it should always be a given because delivering anything less than your best effort may result in having to revisit a project a second or even third time.

KEY TAKEAWAYS

✓ Strive for top quality. It's what sets you apart.

✓ Go the extra mile. It is always worth it.

✓ Quality is nonnegotiable.

✓ Work slower to be faster and do things once.

CASE STUDY

SUMMARY

Setting rules—governance—frees you from constant decision-making. Standards establish boundaries and allow for the measurement of project success and employee performance. The more standards you define and put in place, the fewer scenarios will occur that fall entirely outside your projections. And when you do need to make exceptions to agreed-upon standards, you'll find that some of those exceptions will eventually become standards themselves.

PROBLEM

When a client started with a new data center with no applications in it, they had a unique situation: there was no standard process to review and approve application architectures before applications were installed. This situation presented an important opportunity: they could finally set all of the standards they wanted for the infrastructure that would support their required applications.

SOLUTION

T2 collaborated with a team representing various IT disciplines to set all of the standards that would be implemented. These standards were then communicated to all the project managers working with the multiple application teams in charge of the migration to the new data center. To continuously communicate these standards and make sure they were followed, all application architectures were reviewed and approved during a weekly meeting before any build requests were submitted. This process was followed for the entirety of the project. This operational process was so successful the client decided to adopt it themselves.

Conclusion

LIFE IS A PROJECT BY KEVIN TORF

Undertaking and completing projects has much in common with life itself. The tips in this book were written to show how to be a better project manager, as well as how to adapt and change how you organize teams and manage people in order to be successful. But the very same tips could be applied to how you go about managing life's day-to-day chores.

I have practiced most of these tips throughout my adult life, and I still reflect and make adjustments, as these tips suggest, so that I can adapt to an ever-changing world, my current circumstances, my family, and my work. These tips have taught me to build a framework, that, in turn, has allowed me to achieve what I have intended in every facet of my life and in the projects I have been responsible for.

I have used different metaphors over the last forty years to describe the methods I use to manage large-scale projects. Many of these metaphors have influenced who I have become and what I practice.

Take chess, for instance. Chess is like life. Each chess move has a direct consequence; it can set off a course of action that can be hard to change. The more, however, you can anticipate and plan ahead, the more you can control the consequences. This view can be seen as contradicting the Agile principles and tips suggested in this book. And on the surface, it does. But chess is more about being aware of everything around you, and continually reflecting on your current situation—while always moving forward. So in truth it is *not* that different from the tips herein.

In chess, each move needs an objective, a backup plan, and an understanding of the factors affecting your decision. In addition, your opponent's moves keep changing how you might be playing, similar to the effect of changes in the business and outside world on your project. Understanding these changes and being prepared, detail-oriented, and organized are all elements that will train your mind to adapt quickly.

I have been very fortunate to have worked with many different people over the course of my life who have changed or influenced my thinking. I started my career as a one-dimensional leader—always in control and wanting to do things my way. I was successful in some incredible ways, but I learned over time that my approach did not allow me to grow or scale my thinking. I also learned that there are always multiple ways to look at the same problem and that we all carry different perspectives.

My biggest lesson in this was when I emigrated from South Africa to the United States and tried M&M's, which I did not like. I had grown up eating Smarties, a similar candy from South Africa. During the thirty years I have been in the United States, whenever family members from South Africa visit me, they have always brought me a box of Smarties. One afternoon, I was reading a magazine about an American who had immigrated to South Africa whose only complaint about the country was that Smarties were terrible and he could not wait to have his family send him M&M's. I learned that day that no country or person is better than another. They're just different, and our perceptions of them are based on what we as individuals have grown up to appreciate.

I also learned over time that a team can achieve a lot more than any single person. Sports are a reminder of how this plays out. I am a fan of English football, and in 2015 Leicester City won the Premier League after being promoted from the lower leagues. Leicester City had a salary of only eighty-three million dollars and not a single recognized star player. They competed against some of the most well-funded teams in the world with salaries in excess of three hundred million dollars. With teamwork they accomplished what no handicapper in the world thought possible.

My philosophies have morphed over time, adapting to situations rather than consuming countless hours of planning. This does not mean that you should not be prepared. I have constantly wrestled with finding the right balance between planning and making quick decisions. I like to ask potential employees this question when I interview them: "If you were dropped in the middle of the ocean and were unable to tell where land was, what direction would you swim?"

The answer? The direction isn't important, just as long as you swim. If you don't swim, you will drown eventually. Swimming (doing something) might get you where you need to go, or you might head in the wrong direction. Either way, you'll never know unless you start swimming. As you're swimming, try to learn and adjust course as needed, but don't stop.

Many of the tips shared on these pages align with that philosophy. I hope they provide guidance and another perspective that you find useful in your work and perhaps even in your personal life.

ENDNOTES

PROJECT TRIAGE

1   Nakao, H., Ukai, I., & Kotani, J. (2017). A review of the history of the origin of triage from a disaster medicine perspective. *Acute Medicine & Surgery*, 4(4), 379–384. https://doi.org/10.1002/ams2.293

KEEPING SCORE: METRICS ARE VITAL TO PERFORMANCE

2   Keilman, J. (2013, June 26). With no score, every kid can win. *Chicago Tribune.* https://www.chicagotribune.com/news/ct-xpm-2013-06-26-ct-x-0626-keilman-column -20130626-story.html

ASK YOUR TEAM TO WEIGH IN

3   Hopwood, J. C. (n.d.). *George S. Kaufman Biography.* IMDb. Retrieved April 12, 2021, from http://www.imdb.com/name/nm0442151/bio

DON'T TELL YOUR PEOPLE HOW TO WORK

4   Weiss, J. (Ed.). (2006). *The Quotable Manager: Inspiration for Business and Life.* Gibbs Smith.

5   Shepherd, K. (2010). *The Bite Me School of Management: Taking a Bite out of Conventional Thinking.* Decision Toolbox Press.

DETAILS CAN BE DEVILISH

6   Murray, K. M. E. (2001). *Caught in the Web of Words: James Murray and the Oxford English Dictionary.* Yale University Press.

INSTEAD OF BUSYWORK, GIVE TEAM MEMBERS A PURPOSE

7   Helmus, T., Zimmerman, S., Posard, M., Wheeler, J., Ogletree, C., Stroud, Q., & Harrell, M. (2018). *Life as a Private: A Study of the Motivations and Experiences of Junior Enlisted Personnel in the U.S. Army.* RAND Corporation. https://doi.org/10.7249/RR2252

PLAN FOR MURPHY'S LAW

8   Spark, N. T. (2003). The Fastest Man on Earth. *Improbable Research.* https://www.improbable.com/airchives/paperair/volume9/v9i5/murphy/murphy1.php

JUST START SOMETHING ALREADY!

9   Nixon, R. M. (1962). *Six Crises.* Pocket Books.

STAY ON COURSE WITH MORE FREQUENT REVIEW CYCLES

10   Ost, L. (2020, August 19). *How NIST Helped Hero Pilot Jimmy Doolittle Fly.* NIST. https://www.nist.gov/blogs/taking-measure/how-nist-helped-hero-pilot-jimmy-doolittle-fly

ACCEPT CONSTRAINTS

11   Wolfe, T. (2008). *The Right Stuff.* Vintage Detail.

GO THE DISTANCE ONE STEP AT A TIME

12   McMillan, G. (2017, February 6). The 3 runner types: Do you know your type? *McMillan Running.* https://www.mcmillanrunning.com/runner-types-do-you-know-your-type/

DON'T LET TOOLS USE YOU

13   Rowland, I. D. (2019). Archimedes in Syracuse. In *The Divine Spark of Syracuse* (pp. 57–76). Brandeis University Press. https://doi.org/10.2307/j.ctv102bh9s.7

HONESTY IS ALWAYS THE BEST POLICY

14   Greiman, V. (2010, July 15). The Big Dig: Learning from a Mega Project. *Ask.* https://appel.nasa.gov/wp-content/uploads/2013/04/469423main_ASK_39s_big_dig.pdf

15   Flint, A. (2015, December 29). 10 years later, did the Big Dig deliver? *Boston Globe.* https://www.bostonglobe.com/magazine/2015/12/29/years-later-did-big-dig-deliver/tSb8PIMS4QJUETsMpA7SpI/story.html

KEEP YOUR EYE ON ONE BALL

16   "Diversions." *Outlook Business* 3, no. 2, January 26, 2008.

TARGET PRACTICE

17   Pow, S. (2017). The Last Campaign and Death of Jebe Noyan. *Journal of the Royal Asiatic Society of Great Britain & Ireland*, 27(1), 31–51. https://doi.org/10.1017/S135618631600033X

BE READY FOR THE UNEXPECTED

18 Campbell, J., & Moyers, B. D. (1988). *The Power of Myth* (1st ed). Doubleday.

19 Lucas, G., & Edwards, G. (2005, June 2). George Lucas and the Cult of Darth Vader. *Rolling Stone*. https://www.rollingstone.com/movies/movie-news/george-lucas-and-the-cult-of-darth-vader-247142/

COACH THE TEAM THROUGH CHANGE

20 World Health Organization. (2010, February 24). What is a pandemic? *WHO; World Health Organization*. http://www.who.int/csr/disease/swineflu/frequently_asked_questions/pandemic/en/

EVEN SMALL LOSSES ADD UP

21 Daily Mail. (2015, May 27). The average American loses $6,000 during their lifetime. *Daily Mail*. https://www.dailymail.co.uk/femail/article-3099974/The-average-American-loses-6-000-lifetime-spend-week-searching-missing-belongings.html

ALL IT TAKES IS ONE

22 *Domino Day 2010 afgelast*. (2010, April 23). nu.nl. https://www.nu.nl/binnenland/2233093/domino-day-2010-afgelast.html

23 Onbenkend, K. (2010, February 4). *Spreekbeurt Nederlands Domino Day*. Scholieren.com. https://www.scholieren.com/verslag/spreekbeurt-nederlands-domino-day

KEEP YOUR EGO IN CHECK

24 Helzberg, B. C. (2003). *What I Learned Before I Sold to Warren Buffett*. John Wiley & Sons, Incorporated.

UNDERSTAND YOUR STAKEHOLDER

25 Williamson, P. B. (1982). *Patton's principles: A handbook for managers who mean it!* Simon and Schuster. Page 113.

26 Williamson, P. B. (1982). *Patton's principles: A handbook for managers who mean it!* Simon and Schuster. Page 3.

DON'T CREATE AN AVALANCHE

27 Lagorio-Chafkin, C. (2015, September 15). What Happened to Quirky? *Inc.* https://www.inc.com/christine-lagorio/what-happened-to-quirky.html

28 Diana, C. (2015, December 11). New York bankruptcy judge approves sale of Quirky despite General Electric objections. *Albany Business Review*. https://www.bizjournals .com/albany/news/2015/12/11/bankruptcy-judge-approves-sale-of-quirky-despite.html

29 Hartmans, A. (2017, September 26). Quirky Invention Startup Is Back With New Ownership, New Business Model. *Business Insider*. https://www.businessinsider.com/ quirky-reborn-new-ownership-business-model-2017-9

SYNCHRONIZE THE TEAM

30 Brown, D. J. (2021). *The Boys in the Boat*. Penguin Books Canada.

VISUALIZE TEAM ROLES

31 Martin, G. (n.d.). 'A picture is worth a thousand words'—The meaning and origin of this phrase. *The Phrase Finder*. Retrieved April 14, 2021, from https://www.phrases.org.uk/ meanings/a-picture-is-worth-a-thousand-words.html

BUILD TRUST

32 John Elflein. (2021, April 6). Coronavirus deaths worldwide by country. *Statista*. https://www.statista.com/statistics/1093256/novel-coronavirus-2019ncov -deaths-worldwide-by-country/

33 Selena Simmons-Duffin. (2021, May 13). Poll Finds Public Health Has A Trust Problem. *NPR*. https://www.npr.org/2021/05/13/996331692/poll-finds-public-health-has-a- trust-problem.

ANSWER THE QUESTION!

34 Kevin J. McAuliffe, Jr. (2013, December 8). The story of the NUTS! reply. *US Army*. https://www.army.mil/article/92856/the_story_of_the_nuts_reply

CONTROL YOUR EMOTIONS

35 Welch, J. (2003). *Jack: Straight from the Gut*. Headline. http://archive.org/details/ jackstraightfrom0000welc

KNOW WHEN TO SPEAK UP

36 Gold, H. (1957). The Purity and Cunning of Sherwood Anderson. *The Hudson Review*, 10(4), 548–557. https://doi.org/10.2307/3848918

KNOW YOUR TEAM MEMBERS

37 Bacon, K. (2005, November 29). Master Among Men. *The Atlantic*. https://www.theatlantic.com/magazine/archive/2005/11/master-among-men/304460/

ENTRUST OTHERS WITH RESPONSIBILITY

38 Dickerson, J. (2020). *The Hardest Job in the World: The American Presidency* (First edition). Random House.

BAN SELFISHNESS ON THE TEAM

39 Kets de Vries, M. F. R. (2017, May 10). How to Manage a Narcissist. *Harvard Business Review*. https://hbr.org/2017/05/how-to-manage-a-narcissist

COLLABORATE REGULARLY

40 Reider, B. (2012). The Rashomon Effect. *The American Journal of Sports Medicine*, 1719–1721. https://doi.org/10.1177/0363546512455787

REACH A TEAM CONSENSUS

41 Vuillamy, E. (2001, December 2). Let's Roll . . . *The Guardian*. http://www.theguardian.com/world/2001/dec/02/september11.terrorism1

THE IMPORTANCE OF EFFECTIVE PROCESSES

42 Ford Motor Company. (2010). *The Model T Put the World on Wheels*. http://ophelia.sdsu.edu:8080/ford/02-28-2010/about-ford/heritage/vehicles/modelt/672-model-t.html

DON'T ASSUME: BE CLEAR ABOUT EXPECTATIONS

43 Grossman, L. (2010, November 10). Nov. 10, 1999: Metric Math Mistake Muffed Mars Meteorology Mission. **Wired**. https://www.wired.com/2010/11/1110mars-climate-observer-report/

ADAPT FOR PROJECT SUCCESS

44 Pollan, M. (2006). *The Omnivore's Dilemma: A Natural History of Four Meals*. Penguin Press.

SLOW DOWN TO GO FASTER

45 Gelles, D., Kitroeff, N., Nicas, J., & Ruiz, R. R. (2019, March 23). Boeing Was 'Go, Go, Go' to Beat Airbus With the 737 Max. *The New York Times.* https://www.nytimes.com/2019/03/23/business/boeing-737-max-crash.html

ENHANCE PRODUCTIVITY BY MAKING MEETINGS FUN

46 Espy, L. (2017, February 23). Practicing Leadership Through Dungeons & Dragons. *Project Bliss.* https://projectbliss.net/how-dungeons-dragons-can-prepare-you-for-leadership/

BE THE BEST YOU CAN BE

47 King Jr., M. L. (1967, April 26). *Martin Luther King Jr.: April 26, 1967, Cleveland speech.* https://www.cleveland.com/pdextra/2012/01/martin_luther_king_jr_april_26.html

ABOUT THE AUTHORS

ABOUT T2 TECH GROUP

Since its founding in 2006, T2 Group through T2 Tech has consistently delivered consulting and management advisory services and implemented transformational projects, realizing value-driven results through innovative technologies and quality services for the most prestigious healthcare organizations in the country.

T2's hands-on team includes experienced executives, subject-matter experts, project managers, and business strategists that balance business and IT needs, use a proven project management framework, see projects through from assessment to post-implementation, and practice transparency in everything they do. Unlike many consulting firms, T2 has no financial interest in vendor selection, freeing them to focus completely on realizing client goals. They effectively collaborate with enterprises at all organizational levels, enabling innovations and changes vital to achieving strategic and operational goals. Their range of expertise includes data center strategies, data analytics, security, business continuity, IT operations and financial management.

T2 employs a highly effective hybrid project management methodology that uses PMI-backed waterfall techniques for upfront planning and an agile approach to execution. This unique approach provides the flexibility needed to address changing requirements throughout a project's life cycle and helps teams maintain course to meet the project vision on time and within budget.

ABOUT KEVIN TORF

At fifty-nine, Kevin has collected a portfolio of over eleven companies that he has seen from idea to reality throughout the past forty years. His initial inspiration came from his father, Ronnie, who had an interest in electronics and computer programming as a hobby and brought on young Kevin as an apprentice at the age of thirteen. Armed with his hands-on experience tinkering with electronics with his father, Kevin started his first company, Compu-Video, at the age of nineteen. In 1981, he developed a software program to track and manage a video rental store that included tracking a person's movie preferences and suggesting what they should rent. After selling that software to a large computer company, Kevin then started Netlink, a company reselling and providing professional services networking computers together just at the introduction of the first personal desktop. He sold this company to PunchLine, who in turn sold it to Fintech, the largest telecommunications firm in his home country of South Africa.

Kevin stayed at PunchLine for several years and excelled as the managing director of a new division called Lan Design. This company manufactured customized network solutions for enterprise clients. In 1990 Kevin moved to California with the intention of beginning a new venture. This led to the creation of Torsys, which became a global network consulting firm, providing network solutions to top companies such as Microsoft, Starwood Lodging Worldwide, UCLA, and Packard Bell.

Torsys began as a one-man show, with Kevin running ads in the local Manhattan Beach newspaper offering to fix computers. Through referrals and networking, Kevin started acquiring contracts from companies and grew Torsys to more than one hundred engineers. However, one of the challenges for Kevin was the difficulty of communicating with the engineers stationed all over the world. In order to solve this issue, Kevin developed an internal communications system that collected voice messages and faxes and sent them as emails. This enabled Torsys' employees to consolidate and manage their messages, saving valuable time.

What started as a solution to an internal communications problem at Torsys became the innovative technology and concept behind Kevin's next venture: Tornado Development Inc., Kevin, with the help of the network he built, succeeded in raising ten million dollars in the first round and fifty million dollars total from significant investors, including Intel and GE Capital.

Tornado Development grew over the next five years to more than 150 employees and opened offices in Belgium, London, and Hong Kong. Tornado secured telecommunication giants such as Siemens, Global Crossing, and Verizon as clients. At its height, the company was valued at around 300 million dollars. Despite the promising technology and backing from top-tier companies, Tornado could not shield itself from the tech bubble that burst in the early 2000s.

Looking back, Kevin recalls several lessons learned from Tornado's collapse beyond unfortunate timing. First, Tornado offered a technology ahead of its time, and the team underestimated the difficulty, time, and cost of acquiring and maintaining a solid user base.

Kevin spent almost a year negotiating to buy Tornado's intellectual property back from the investors. In the meantime, he started two other companies, Reaction Labs and SportsPal, that provided web hosting and software development services to help manage sports teams' schedules and travel for top brands around the world.

In 2003, once Kevin secured Tornado's IP, he partnered with Belkin International to start another company called iNuntius Inc. This company focused on selling VoIP technology platforms to enterprise clients and consumers. This was the first commercial digital phone service of its kind. The partnership with Belkin provided the credibility and distribution channels in order for iNuntius to succeed, and in 2005 Intelliverse bought the company.

Kevin worked at Intelliverse for two years, but the entrepreneur in him still yearned to express his creativity and start a new venture. Fortuitously, in 2008, a former client and friend asked him to consult on a project managing the information technology system at a hospital. From this project, Kevin and his partner, Robert Konishi, identified a need in the healthcare sector for improving IT systems, and T2 Technology Group was born.

Around the same time, Kevin came up with another business idea. While trying to keep track of all the sports bets he and his son, Kyle, made in Vegas during March Madness, Kevin knew he could create a better technological solution to the problem. He developed the Bet Tracker mobile app, which managed users' sports bets and tracked sporting events from around the world. At its height, Bet Tracker had over 250,000 users through the Apple and Android stores. Kevin sold this company in 2017.

T2 Group has grown over the last fifteen years and now includes T2 Tech, T2 Labs, T2 Flex, T2 eHealth, and T2 Dev. All five companies provide services to the leading hospital systems in the country. T2 Tech provides project management and oversight for large-scale, multimillion dollar projects for hospitals and healthcare providers. T2 Flex offers comprehensive patient scheduling, managing several hundred thousand appointments and coordinating appointments across multiple hospital departments. T2 Labs provides turnkey lab testing that is needed for a hospital to expand its capabilities to support all forms of health testing. T2 Dev builds software solutions to facilitate the management of IT infrastructure and work from home technology tools for the healthcare industry. T2 eHealth is Kevin's latest expansion of the T2 Group, offering an e-commerce platform for hospital systems and providers for different forms of at home testing and healthcare products.

Kevin attributes much of his entrepreneurial success to the core principles he lives by. He is adamant about providing the best quality service to his customers—so that if a contract is not fulfilled to his standard of quality, he will not accept payment until his customers are satisfied. Throughout the years, his commitment to excellence and hard work has earned him the respect of his peers and clients. In fact, contrary to other consulting firms, T2 provides an at-will contract that gives the client the ability to terminate the agreement at any time.

With one exception, Kevin has single-handedly built his companies from an idea into profitable businesses. Today, T2 employs more than 120 people. Kevin attributes this accomplishment first to the support of his wonderful wife, Sue, who has been instrumental in the creation and execution of many of his late-night ideas, and second to his approach and philosophy, outlined in this book.